Words of recommendation for *Getting Ready for Baptism*

At last, a great resource for families and congregations to enable the exploration of the meaning and symbolism of baptism.

Baptism is such a significant step on anyone's journey of faith, and this course book celebrates the occasion and explores its deeper spiritual significance. It can easily be used with individuals and small groups, across a wide range of ages. I would recommend that every church has adequate supplies of this resource for all who come seeking baptism.

ROBERT WESTON, MINISTER IN READING, BERKSHIRE, AND CONVENER OF THE UNITED REFORMED CHURCH YOUTH AND CHILDREN'S WORK COMMITTEE (2009–2013)

D0993187

Text copyright © Richard Burge, Penny Fuller and Mary Hawes 2014
The authors assert the moral right
to be identified as the authors of this work

Published by
The Bible Reading Fellowship
15 The Chambers, Vineyard
Abingdon OX14 3FE
United Kingdom
Tel: +44 (0)1865 319700
Email: enquiries@brf.org.uk
Website: www.brf.org.uk
BRF is a Registered Charity

ISBN 978 0 85746 019 6

First published 2014
10 9 8 7 6 5 4 3 2 1 0
All rights reserved

Acknowledgments
Unless otherwise stated, scripture quotations are taken from the Contemporary English Version of the Bible published by HarperCollins Publishers, copyright © 1991, 1992, 1995 American Bible Society.

Scripture quotations taken from the Holy Bible, New International Version (Anglicised edition), copyright © 1979, 1984, 2011 by Biblica, are used by permission of Hodder & Stoughton Publishers, an Hachette UK company. All rights reserved. 'NIV' is a registered trademark of Biblica. UK trademark number 1448790.

Cover photo: Hemera/Thinkstock

A catalogue record for this book is available from the British Library

Printed in the UK by MWL

Getting Ready for Baptism

Course Book

Richard Burge, Penny Fuller and Mary Hawes

Important Information

Photocopying permission

The right to photocopy material in *Getting Ready for Baptism* is granted for the pages that contain the photocopying clause: 'Reproduced with permission from *Getting Ready for Baptism* by Richard Burge, Penny Fuller and Mary Hawes (Barnabas for Children, 2014)', so long as reproduction is for use in a teaching situation by the original purchaser. The right to photocopy material is not granted for anyone other than the original purchaser without written permission from BRF.

The Copyright Licensing Agency (CLA)

If you are resident in the UK and you have a photocopying licence with the Copyright Licensing Agency (CLA) please check the terms of your licence. If your photocopying request falls within the terms of your licence, you may proceed without seeking further permission. If your request exceeds the terms of your CLA licence, please contact the CLA directly with your request. Copyright Licensing Agency, Saffron House, 6–10 Kirby Street, London EC1N 8TS. Telephone 020 7400 3100; fax 020 7400 3101; email cla@cla.co.uk; website www.cla.co.uk. The CLA will provide photocopying authorisation and royalty fee information on behalf of BRF.

BRF is a Registered Charity (No. 233280)

Contents

Introduction

A baptism is often thought of as the starter before the party begins: the celebration *after* the church bit is considered to be the real celebration. We have taken the concept of party and used it as a theme throughout the book—celebration at a party where God, the baptismal candidate, parents, families, friends and church families celebrate and embrace the sacrament of baptism together as a community.

Baptism is a once-in-a-lifetime moment, something that can never be repeated. It is a unique and special occasion, a reason to rejoice. People can be baptised at any age: for some, it is a decision made by their parents when they are very young; for others, it may be a choice they are allowed to make themselves and choose to be baptised as they are growing up. You are never too old to be baptised, and whenever you are baptised, it is a very special time.

In baptism, people start something new. Baptism is an occasion filled with symbolism and meaning. It is about birth and death and new life; it is about being made clean—as good as new; it is about becoming part of a new family—the people of God, the church; it is about the person being baptised; it is about God, family, the church and being part of a community of people.

Baptism is a gift from God, given so that we can celebrate our life and our journey with God. On the day of the baptism, it can feel as though there is a lot going on and that it is up to us to organise it all, but we should always remember that the real host of this baptism party is God, who rejoices as one of his children comes to baptism.

Preparation for a baptism is a time to celebrate and prepare for the party; *Getting Ready for Baptism* explores what this means. You can use this resource to explore baptism as an individual, in a house group setting, as part of a children's or youth group or as a church leader looking for fresh ways to develop your ministry.

This book gives a wealth of ideas for baptism services and for preparing those who come to church for baptism. There will be far too much to put into one baptism, but take what you need for the day itself and keep the rest for the moment when you will need it. The baptism service lasts for a few minutes, but it is the start of a journey that will last a lifetime.

Structure and layout

Baptism is not just another task in church life; preparation for it requires much more than simply a collection of resources and techniques. *Getting Ready for Baptism* may be used to prepare a member for baptism in families, all-age worship groups, Sunday groups or Sunday school. It is written as a three-session course, which could be held all on one day or split over three separate sessions. The key aim is to inspire people about the wonders of baptism and to nurture the skills and tools that will enable them as they travel on their journey of discipleship.

Part 1: Baptism as a ministry

Part 1 explores baptism as a ministry—the biblical and theological context and the three elements that are involved in the baptism celebration. It also explores how, in baptism, we and God celebrate and respond together in a once-in-a-lifetime sacramental act of faith.

Part 2: The practicalities

Part 2 offers ideas and tools to explore with those asking questions about baptism or preparing for baptism. It is split into three sessions:

- Session 1: Come to the party! (The preparation needed before the event)
- Session 2: Enjoy the party! (The baptism itself)
- Session 3: Party on! (Living as a disciple after baptism)

Each session offers activities to choose from, which are set out like a menu. Use the planning sheet in Appendix 1 to choose the activities you want to focus on and plan your session. The 'menus' (including starter, main course and dessert) contain activities that may be appropriate for the following settings:

- meeting families
- children's groups
- TV dinner: 30-minute home visit

- all-age service ideas
- Sunday group course on baptism

Starters

This will help you to introduce the topics and themes of the main course and give you a good lead in to the main course subject.

Main course

This is the centrepiece: the other courses will be chosen around it. There is a variety of main courses to choose from, and each one helps you to focus on a specific element or theme of baptism.

Desserts

These are activities that will enable the family or candidate to consider issues further or develop skills and tools to use beyond the baptism, to nurture discipleship.

Planning

See Appendix 1 for a planning sheet designed to help you think through which activities you will choose, how long you will want to spend on them and what equipment you may need. There are also a few questions to help you reflect on the session immediately after you have completed it, while it is still fresh in your mind. This may be a useful tool in planning further sessions.

Note: Many of the activities can easily be modified for different settings (including all-age services, parent and toddler groups, or a meeting in a family's living room). We have made suggestions throughout to help you engage creatively with your own group.

My Baptism Journey Activity Book

This journal should be seen as an integral part of the journey of discovering and understanding baptism. It will help children to build the skills of reflective practice as well as embedding faith exploration as part of their church and home life.

PART 1

Baptism as a ministry

The party theme

Baptism generally consists of a threefold requirement:

- Promises are made by the candidate (or by baptised adults on behalf of a candidate who cannot speak for themselves).
- The candidate is signed with the sign of the cross, the sign of Christ.
- The candidate is baptised with water.

However, within these three basic elements there are many variations, and other elements may also be added to the baptism service, depending on your tradition. For example:

- The sign of the cross may be made, with or without oil.
- The baptism may be carried out with a small sprinkling of water or it may involve full immersion in a baptismal pool.
- Lit candles may be given to candidates to depict the journey from darkness to light.
- Oil of chrism may be used, adding fragrant scent to the symbolism of being chosen by God.
- In some services, the signing of the cross is done only by the minister; in others, parents and godparents may also be invited to sign the candidate with the cross, adding a sense of involvement and personal significance to the role they play on the day.
- In some churches, infant candidates may be taken round the church so that the whole congregation can share in the welcome of the child.
- Occasionally, godparents may give a short speech to say how they hope their godchild will grow and develop in life and in faith.

It is not only the elements of the service that are variable. The time and location of the service may also vary greatly:

- Sometimes, a baptism takes place in the main Sunday service; at other times, it may be at a special service for the baptism alone.
- The baptism may be done in the sea, in a river or outside in a pool.
- The entire service may be held around the font in a church, or different parts

may be carried out at significant places in and around the font, with the congregation moving from place to place.

There may be requirements for individual church practice. However, even taking these into account, the variety seems almost endless and it is exciting to see the myriad alternatives that surround this one service of baptism. After all, if every baptism service were exactly the same, it would be like eating the same meal over and over again. *Getting Ready for Baptism* opens wide the store cupboard and encourages churches to explore the various options on the baptismal menu while being aware of their own particular traditions.

Planning for the party

Baptism is a ministry and a celebration like no other. At this baptism party, there may be different people involved in the planning and delivery:

The person who meets the baptism family to talk to them about the baptism may be the minister or a lay person, preparing the family for this great moment and explaining the things that will happen in the church on the day. Perhaps they will explore the symbolism of the service and the wonderful mystery of this great celebration. This may happen in a meeting where lots of baptism families are brought together or it may be a 15-minute meeting with a family in their own living-room.

- **Question:** What opportunities are there in your setting to talk and share about baptism?

A volunteer or paid worker with a church or project may wish to explore what baptism means with the children in their group on Sunday or midweek. Alternatively, they may have been asked by a parent of a child in their group whether they do baptisms at the church.

- **Question:** How can children and young people in your setting learn more about the meaning of baptism?

Parents may bring a child for baptism. *Godparents* may be chosen for their friendship, their faith and/or because they are a family member. They should be enabled to fulfil the promises we ask them to make on behalf of the candidate; this may be the means by which God enables them to grow in faith too.

- **Question:** How can you support parents and godparents in your setting?

A child may see a baptism in the church service or attend a family member's baptism and ask questions about what it means.

- **Question:** How can you help younger children in your setting to understand the meaning of the baptism services they attend?

The person at the centre of the baptism is *the candidate* who is to be baptised. They may be a newborn, infant or older child. The candidate may have been adopted, and baptism may hold special significance for them as part of a new start and family identity. A new understanding of faith may bring older candidates to request baptism. Sometimes the request comes from someone who seeks baptism, having seen others do the same. Whatever the reason, it is important to recognise the journey that has brought the candidate for baptism. Baptism is a means by which God meets with and touches people, and we are privileged to share in this ministry, mission and sacrament.

• **Question:** What opportunities do you offer in your setting to baptism candidates, to help them prepare for baptism and a life of faith?

The preparation and the baptism service give an opportunity to explore, with those who hold these important roles, the responsibilities they are taking as well as the meaning and significance of baptism, faith and the Christian journey.

Baptism is:
• a celebration and a sacrament
• a gift from God
• a once-in-a-lifetime occasion

Questions
• How many baptisms happen at your church each year?
• What percentage of baptisms are people who have had some relationship with your church?
• What percentage of your baptismal candidates are new to your church and do not regularly attend?
• What attracts people to come to your church for a baptism?
• What opportunities are there in your church setting to explore the ministry of baptism?

You may wish to complete the reflection sheet in Appendix 2. Copies can be downloaded from www.barnabasinchurches.org.uk/9780857460196 for use with different sessions.

Preparing for the party

Let us focus on some of the opportunities that might arise during the preparation for a baptism.

For the church family

There are opportunities to live out our ministry through baptism. Families come to baptism for many and various reasons, and many people—through the welcome they receive and the joy, celebration and wonder at the love of God in baptism—then find a home in the church.

Being present at a baptism is a high calling and a great responsibility. It is mission that comes to us on a plate! In baptism, God receives people, whoever they are. The service and the baptism celebration should be filled with hospitality and welcome. Those attending should be made to feel at home, for the welcome of the church is a glimpse of the welcoming hospitality of God. They are welcomed in the name of God and will not forget the way they are treated in the church on the day of the baptism.

Those attending will make promises to nurture the baptism candidates in the way of God and as part of the church; these are important promises and should be taken seriously. Although the day of the baptism is a one-off occasion, baptism kick-starts a journey on which people seek to follow God and to live a life where God is central to all they do.

For those involved in children's, youth and family ministry

Baptism is a great opportunity to explore the many aspects of our belief in God during our sessions with children and young people. Some of the children and young people may not have been baptised and may start asking questions about it. Young families in your ministry may be uncertain whether to baptise their child, leading to opportunities to discuss baptism.

Sometimes, children and young people ask big questions, such as 'What is heaven?' or 'What does God promise?' Baptism gives us a way in to talk about all this. The forthcoming baptism of a baby may lead to questions about the wonder of creation. Children may ask why water is used in baptism, giving an opportunity to explore the symbolism. Baptism may be an opportunity to think about Jesus' life, his infancy, his childhood and his own baptism. Discussions about baptism can also lead to more general questions about life, death and resurrection.

The *My Baptism Journey Activity Book* can be used by children to explore what they think and feel about baptism.

Questions
- Take some time to reflect on how, in your ministry, you can engage with mission opportunities that arise through exploration of baptism.
- What opportunities are there in your context to explore baptism with the different groupings in your church (for example, children, young people and families)?

Work through the questions on the reflection sheet in Appendix 2.

Party planning: going deeper

The biblical background to baptism

At the very start of Mark's Gospel (Mark 1:9–11), we read that Jesus was baptised. We read in Matthew's Gospel (Matthew 3) of how Jesus went to the River Jordan and met with John the Baptist, a cousin of Jesus, who was baptising people in the waters of the river and had been doing so for some time. John believed that Jesus should baptise him (Matthew 3:14), but Jesus had come to be baptised by John. The waters of cleansing were not a New Testament idea, but, when Jesus was baptised, something new began: he was not only baptised in water but he was also baptised by the Holy Spirit (Matthew 3:16–17).

The early church was quick to begin the practice of baptism as a rite of passage for those entering into 'the Way' (the name first given to Christianity as a faith). People marked a start to their new life by baptism, sometimes as individuals and sometimes as whole households. Jews and Gentiles all came to begin their new way of life in Christ through baptism.

Our traditions have been passed on through church history since the days of the early church (as described in the book of Acts). The sacrament of baptism is full of tradition and custom, but at its heart there is a biblical foundation reaching back to the day when Jesus waded out into the waters of the River Jordan.

> **Questions**
> - How can we make the story of John baptising Jesus relevant for baptism groups?
> - What is the significance of this story?
>
> Work through the questions on the reflection sheet in Appendix 2.

God is at the centre

Many baptisms centre on the child or candidate to be baptised, and God can sometimes become an 'extra' in the occasion or forgotten about for a while. In fact, though, God is at the heart of what is going on at baptism. God has already shown his love for this candidate, and the baptism is a symbol of God's grace.

Baptism is a response to the love of God in the presence of God among the people of God.

The following activities will help you to explore this idea (perhaps individually, as you prepare yourself to lead a baptism group; or within a group context, maybe of other church leaders who are preparing candidates for baptism; or within your baptism group, as part of their preparation).

 ## Starter

Bible characters  **Allow 10 minutes**

You will need:
Enough copies of Appendix 3; scissors; pens

Cut up the different sections of the sheets. (You will need one set for each subgroup, if appropriate.) Spread the cards out on a tabletop or floor, and ask the subgroups (or individuals) to choose different stories to focus on. Provide some blank cards for people to note down their responses on, if they want to.

 ## Main course

Descriptions of baptism 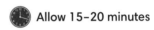 **Allow 15–20 minutes**

You will need:
Enough copies of Appendix 4; a roll of wallpaper lining paper; art materials; newspaper to cover flooring and furnishings

Hand out the copies of Appendix 4, explaining that these are a number of other links and references to baptism in a biblical context.

Spread the lining paper across a table or the floor and place the art materials around it. Read the paragraphs of information on Appendix 4 and use the questions to help you express your thoughts.

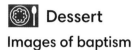 ## Dessert

Images of baptism  **Allow 10–15 minutes**

You will need:
Enough copies of Appendix 5.

Look at the images in Appendix 5. Where can you see the symbols of baptism? What do the images say to you?

The centrality of God in baptism is highlighted in a traditional medieval French baptism prayer:

[Name], for you Christ came, for you he fought and he suffered. For you he entered the shadow of the garden in Gethsemane and the horror of the cross on Calvary. For you he fought and he suffered, for you he died and rose again. For you he ascended into heaven and there he has been praying for you even before you knew it. In this way the word of the gospel has come true. 'We love him because he first loved us.'

In baptism, it is God who blesses the child with water as a ritual act of washing; it is God who holds the child in his arms; it is God who anoints with oil; it is God's light that shines in the darkness. It is because of God's joy and celebration at this event that the angels rejoice so much in heaven.

Baptism is an act of community

A party is a celebration within one community, made up of people from many communities, who come together to form another community at the event.

On almost every occasion, baptism takes place within a community. For example, in the Church of England and the Methodist Church, it is expected that baptism will take place within the community of the main Sunday morning service of the church. Here, the newly baptised member is welcomed within the context of the community of which they have become a part, and the community celebrates together the newest of their members. The act is intrinsically about community.

A major part of the role that godparents or sponsors play in baptism comes from this act of community. They make promises from within the community for those who are too young to make the promises for themselves, and are there to guide and walk with the newly baptised person as they grow, to lead them into the Christian community, encouraging them on their discipleship journey.

In the biblical account of Philip and the Ethiopian (Acts 8:26–39), we see only the baptised person and the baptiser present (and, indeed, in emergency baptisms today the same limited number may be present), but this does not remove the imperative that baptism brings a person into a wider community of believers. Indeed, even in the largest service where a baptism takes place, the visible community will be only a glimpse of the community into which the candidate has been baptised. The size of the baptised community covers the whole globe and all times past, present and future.

Baptism is an act of faith and trust

Baptism is a sacrament—that is, a symbolic representation of an invisible and imperceptible grace. In baptism, the candidate is symbolically washed clean and born again; the candidate declares their belief in God at the moment of their baptism and promises to walk with Christ.

These actions call to mind the deep and real impact of baptism in the life of the candidate. The sacrament of baptism signifies a life-changing moment, the impact of which we trust God for in faith. We believe that in baptism the relationship between God and the newly baptised person is nurtured. Like a seed that has the potential for growth, it is almost the mystical moment of germination, unseen and beyond our ability. In baptism, we trust God and expect the community to provide all the support and strength that are needed to enable the life after baptism to be one of growth and development.

Baptism is traditional

From the baptism of Christ in the earliest Gospels through to the traditions of the early church in the book of Acts and the early church writings, we see the value that was initially placed on baptism. Even in its earliest days, the Church began to develop a tradition and expectation of baptism.

In early church writings, such as the first/second-century *Didache*, we can see in some detail how the traditions around the act of baptism were developing to signify the meaning of baptism to those observing and those being baptised.

There were times when baptism took place only on Easter Day, after a great time of preparation. This tradition enabled the candidates to experience in a remarkable way the symbolism of being buried with Christ and being born again into his risen life.

From these early beginnings, although its practice has changed significantly, baptism has always remained a tradition within the church. Through all the schisms and division, through reformation and through revolution, baptism has always been at the heart of Christian practice and doctrine.

More than that, even in our society, which is seen by some as being post-Christian, baptism is still seen as a tradition. Many families come to churches each year to have the baby christened, to undertake the ritual of baptism, the traditional action of completing the celebration of new birth.

Baptism is a significant moment

Baptisms may be small, personal, family occasions or they may be a day when extended families gather in a church, bedecked in all their finery. This is all part of the day of celebration and the events happening after the service itself. The effort that people make in getting ready for the day, and the significance they place upon it, should not be ignored. Within the church we should embrace it: it is indeed a significant moment, a celebration of the goodness of God and a celebration of family and community. It is an important and memorable day for young and old. As a church, we should work with this value and seek to develop the other areas of significance.

For those who are old enough to make the promises themselves, the day and the moment of baptism may be deeply meaningful and memorable. For parents and godparents of younger candidates, the same significance should be nurtured. Whoever makes the promises on the day of the baptism is declaring something truly significant, and they must be enabled to recognise its meaning.

On the day of the baptism, they will declare their belief in God and they will recognise the desire to walk with God in their lives. The future may hold all sorts of things, good and bad. However, one of the gifts of baptism is to enable those making the promises to experience a memorable and significant moment when those words are true. It can be a moment of faith and a touchstone of hope throughout their lives. They may find it hard to recognise the same belief at times in the future; indeed, they may forget its significance over time, but we should enable them to experience and rejoice in that moment when they declare the words of faith on the day of the baptism.

Baptism is permanent

When someone is baptised, it is a once-in-a-lifetime moment. People may renew their baptismal promises but they can never be baptised for a second time. There are times when people may be baptised conditionally, if it is not known whether they have been baptised already, but even here the words 'if you have not been baptised already' are added. Baptism can only happen once in a person's life.

The church does not make this condition as a means of keeping baptism special; it is not intended to make administration simple or to keep down the numbers coming to ask for baptism in the church. Baptism is a unique moment because its effects can never be taken away.

At baptism, the relationship between God and the baptised person comes into a new focus. The relationship between God and the candidate has always been important to God, but in baptism the relationship is reciprocated and a stronger bond is formed through the love returned.

Many biblical images spring to mind about this stronger relationship—stories of sheep being brought into the fold, new people being brought into the family, children being adopted and the image of our name being engraved (or tattooed) on to the hand of God.

In baptism, we enter through a door into a new way of relationship with God. While our understanding of God and of the significance of baptism may develop or diminish, God's love for us is not changed by our love for him. Our name is still tattooed on his hand; we are still sheep in his flock and, as the good shepherd, he searches for us and longs to bring us back when we wander.

Baptism is important

All the above descriptions of baptism highlight its importance. It was important in the life of Christ; it is important in the life of the church; it is important to the church community; it is important in the family and in our society, and it is important to those being baptised. This great importance highlights the opportunities for the church community to welcome and support those being baptised as well as the parents and godparents who speak for those too young to speak for themselves.

The party guest list

A baptism may be a small family affair around a font, or it may be a large celebration in a gathering of thousands. Essentially, though, there are three core groups at any baptism, three elements coming together in celebration.

- God
- The candidate (and perhaps their family and friends)
- The church family

God

God is very much the host of the baptism. It was through the actions of God, even before the date of the baptism was set, that the momentum towards the special day began.

The baptism is a sacramental action by which the candidate accepts and responds to the love that God has shown since before they were born. It is this response of the candidate that sends the angels into party mode in heaven (Luke 15:10), and the Spirit of God hosts the baptismal party as a celebration on earth.

Whether or not he is acknowledged by all those at the service, God is present. A lack of belief cannot negate the presence of God and the joy of God as an individual turns to Christ.

The candidate, their family and friends

Next to God, the candidate is the second crucial element of the baptismal party. With no candidate, there would be no baptism, and, while it is the individual who is being baptised, they will often bring with them their family and friends.

Small children will by necessity come with their parents or guardians, and godparents will form a wider family group. Older candidates may determine to request baptism on their own volition, but they may well have formed that opinion within a supportive group of friends.

So to the party come the candidate, their family and their friends. This may be a small group of a parent and three godparents, or it may be a church full.

The church family

A baptism can take place in isolation, but the very essence of baptism is that the candidate is baptised into the family of the people of God. At the very least, this element of the baptismal guest list will be seen in the minister who performs the baptism, but ideally there should be representatives of the worshipping community to welcome the new member into the church family and into the community of the faithful.

Models of a baptism

Equal and dynamic community

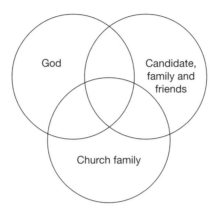

This 'baptismal trinity' shows a coming together of the three parties at a great celebration. Each has a vital role in the celebration, forming an energetic interaction of relationships and community.

However, this model of an equal and dynamic community is not always the reality of our baptismal experience. Many of us will have been part of services that display a very different dynamic.

Non-contact baptism

Here, the three elements arrive at the baptism but there is a lack of communication and engagement between them. Sometimes the congregation will fail to be welcoming to the baptismal party. They may not necessarily be unwelcoming but may appear indifferent. The congregation may give the signal to the 'visitors' that they are outsiders. Even when the church tries hard to make a concerted effort to welcome families coming for baptism, the same dynamic can be created. The welcome can highlight and reinforce the message that there is a difference between those who are within the church family and those who are incomers. It is a careful balance to strike.

Perhaps it is hard to see the 'God' circle here separated from the 'church family'. It is to be hoped that the church family is always connected to God, and it is certainly true that God is always connected to people, but the separation highlights that the actions of the congregation can show a very different form from the love that God shows to the baptismal candidate, their family and friends. The idea of separation between the church family and God may be a hard pill for us to swallow, but it is not an uncommon reality in the practice of a significant number of church members.

The separation also highlights that, for a truly shared celebration of baptism, the church congregation needs to see those who enter the church as if they were looking through the eyes of God. The love of God has been shown equally to all humanity, and all come before him on equal terms in worship. No one is more worthy because of their own goodness. Only through God's grace do any of us come into the presence of God.

The separation between baptism families and God is something that many would see as very common. While there are certainly many who come for baptism through a sense of conviction and faith, a very significant number of people come to baptism because they are following a family and social tradition. Others may want their child to experience something they experienced as a child, and some people may be on the start of a journey, asking questions and thinking about something wider than their own existence.

Although the church community can, by their actions, separate themselves from the likeness of a God who is always connected to them, God, through the presence of the Holy Spirit, is always working among people. God works in the world among people who have no desire to believe. How much more should we remember and anticipate God's desire to touch and engage with those who come forward? The actions of those coming to the service may cause the circles to repel one another, but they can never overpower the love of God, which attracts them.

Baptism at a tangent

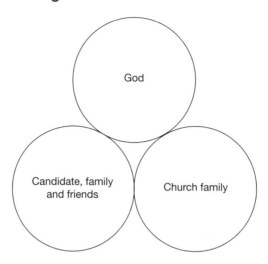

Here, there is no separation between church family and the baptism family, but the contact is only at arm's length. The congregation have a desire to bring the candidate and their family and friends to meet with God, to be touched by the community of the church family, but it is to be a fleeting visit. There is no desire for real interaction and fellowship. Like the seeds on the rocky ground in the parable of the farmer (Luke 8:4–15), the experience for those coming for baptism is important but not long-lasting.

There is little preparation of the candidates and their family for baptism in this setting, and the follow-up, too, will be limited. It may be that the congregation and church give the baptism family a few opportunities to deepen their relationship with God and the church, but those opportunities are in the form of hoops and challenges rather than real support to start a journey of discipleship.

The dynamics of a community in baptism

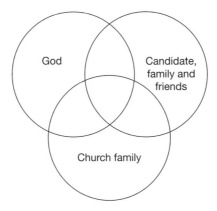

This brings us back to the 'trinity of baptism'. In this model of baptism dynamics, the church meets with God—a crucial aim of the church every time it gathers for worship, for fellowship or for any reason. People should be gathering together with an expectation, an anticipation that they will engage with God. We should be gathering ready to attend to God, ready to be filled with joy and wonder as we renew our awareness that God is among his people by his Spirit. We come as ourselves, but by God's grace we are lifted to join the celebrations of heaven. Our worship should be a reflection of the celebrations we read about that fill the heavenly halls (see, for example, Revelation 19:5–10).

A baptism service is an opportunity for the people of God to gather in anticipation and joy that we will dance with God. Our dance may not always be happy; we may hold much sadness or many troubles in our hearts, but we can always be joyful, mindful that in God we can overcome all things.

It is into this community that the candidate and their family will enter. They come never as outsiders but as those who share the same opportunity to experience the grace of God—the dynamic of God's love that takes hold of people before they know it. Members of the baptism party may not have responded to it yet, but they have been blessed with the same love of God that he has shown in Christ, who died and rose for all people. In a baptism service, the God who loved us first should be tangible to all who are present. The baptism party should be a celebration equally for the newcomer and for those who have known this wonderful news for many years.

It should not be overlooked that the interaction of the 'God' circle and the 'candidate and family' circle will have been active before the service. God does not wait for people to come into church before he takes an interest in them. There is much opportunity for God's Spirit to have been at work, and any preparation before the service should join in with this part of the dance. Likewise, at the service and after the service, our ministry will enable the candidate especially, and their family, to continue in the engagement with God that the baptism has brought to their awareness.

The heart of the party

In our three models, the heart of the party is the point where all three circles meet and form a place of community. It is only when God, the church fellowship and the candidate and family engage and celebrate together that they can really feel God at the centre of that community.

This is why baptism is so important in the mission of the church. Baptism is worship, mission, wonder and celebration. It is the experience of God at work in the world. If we treat baptism with a sense of tiredness and routine, we withdraw ourselves from the party.

The wonderful ministry of baptism should inspire us afresh and ensure that God and people can come together in worship to celebrate. It should also enthuse the people of God in their ministry of fellowship and community, and enable those who come to the church to support the candidates to be inspired and touched by the love of God that is celebrated in baptism.

Questions
- Think about baptisms in your context. Which of the models do they most resemble?
- What could you introduce into your baptism preparation that would enable the three elements to weave more closely together?

Use the reflection sheet in Appendix 2 to write your answers.

PART 2

The practicalities

— SESSION 1 —

Come to the party!

Session aim

To explore preparation for baptism: who is involved and what coming to the party means to all involved.

Setting the scene

Baptism is a party—a celebration and welcome for the newest member of the family of God. While the baptism itself will be the most important day, preparation is always important. The preparation time for this special event will set the tone and enable those who attend the baptism service to appreciate the day and its symbolism.

The hosts

The earthly host for baptism is the local church and congregation on behalf of God, who is the heavenly host. In effect, the church is hosting God's party. A good host helps people to feel welcome and at ease, and also helps guests to make connections, ensuring that they know what is happening and when. This is an important role in making the party a success, and as such the whole church plays a role in the party. In this book, you will find ideas, conversation starters and activities for use with the congregation; these will help to prepare the congregation to engage with the party and see it as an aspect of mission in the church.

Children rarely have the chance to explore and understand their own baptism or to ask questions about what baptism is. The ideas, activities and discussions outlined here can be used with Sunday or midweek groups to help the children discover what baptism means for them.

Baptism is full of meaning. This great wealth of meaning allows us to choose the elements we feel are most appropriate in each setting; it also enables us to vary the aspects of baptism that we focus on each time. This helps to keep delivery of baptism preparation fresh, and it continually reminds us of the miraculous wonder of baptism.

The community

Baptism is about belonging to a family (we are children of God) and becoming a member of a community (the church, the people of God). Baptism is a rite of passage in which the candidate is initiated, introduced and welcomed as a full member of the body of Christ. In preparation for baptism, a family or candidate may take time to consider the benefits and responsibilities of this new church membership.

As well as recognising the start of church membership, baptism is also very much about the place of a person within their family. Especially when the candidate is an infant, a baptism will often be a family day. It may be one of the few occasions when an extended family gathering takes place. Baptism is an opportunity to enable the family to rejoice in this celebration and to think about the wider human and church family connections it brings, alongside their own place in their family.

The love of God

In baptism we recognise the love of God, which is for all people. Baptism is a gift of grace, something not earned but a gift freely given. It is important that preparation for baptism never gives the impression that people must 'earn' the right to be baptised, or that they need to achieve a particular standard before they can be good enough for the baptism. Baptism is less about us being baptised and more about God's love washing over us. Our part is a response to that love rather than God's love being a reaction to our request. Preparation for baptism is an opportunity to explore the love of God.

For parents with small children, this may be something they have glimpsed in childbirth and in the love that they feel for the new human being they hold. This child cannot earn their love, but they give their love freely and unconditionally, and they will rejoice when the baby responds to their love. This is an insight into the overwhelming love of God and our response to him in baptism.

When the baptism candidate is a baby, the themes of birth and creation may be a very natural starting point. The birth of a new baby is a miraculous event in which we share in the wonder of creation. It is very easy to consider the way that baptism, too, is about being born into a new life and being made a new creation.

This may not be so obvious a link for those who are older, but it is a key element of the preparation for baptism. The sense of starting again and being made new is a powerful image and can be a very helpful part of preparation for an older candidate.

New birth is a biblical phrase that describes very well what happens at baptism. Adoption, too, is used in the Bible as a description of how we become God's adopted children (see, for example, John 1:12; Romans 8:14–16; Galatians 4:4–6). It is a wonderful image and can often be helpful for those who are older when they prepare for baptism. For those who have been adopted, it can also be an illustration and theme that is easy to associate with.

The time of getting ready is a time of great value and foundation. It is a time to create memories that can be revisited in the years to come. Preparing for baptism is like preparing for a great party.

Session activities

The activities, ideas and discussion starters in this session have been designed to help you create a baptism menu that will work for your particular setting. Each main course explores one of the many themes of baptism. We have indicated which mains are more suitable for children's, all-age or adult-focused groups.

There is also a variety of suggestions for appropriate starters and desserts to open up and conclude the session. These are designed to complement the main course: the starters lead into its theme with an activity, while the desserts pull together thoughts at the end.

Think of each of these elements as part of a menu. They can be combined to create an à la carte session or conversation appropriate for the people you are with and the setting you are in. No two baptism preparation sessions will look exactly the same—and remember, you don't need to try out everything on the menu in one go. Use the planning sheet (Appendix 1) to help you.

Sometimes there will be situations where a full menu isn't possible—perhaps a meeting with the family in between the children's teatime and bedtime. The 'coffee conversations' are designed to open up discussion where time is short but you still wish to pursue thoughts and reflections on the significance of baptism.

 Main course

Option 1:
God's family tree

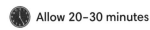 Allow 20–30 minutes

You will need:
Story cards (see Appendix 6); blank cards; flipchart paper; felt-tip pens

This activity can be used with a group of children/adults, just one or two children/ adults or as part of a sermon illustration, to explore our relationship with God and how we become part of the body of Christ when we are baptised. It is also an excellent activity for the whole church and could be used on All Saints' Day or Bible Sunday. It is filled with information and learning but also spiced with wonder and opportunities for discussion when considering why people should be placed where in the tree. The activity also covers many different aspects of baptism—belonging, community, adoption and the words of baptism.

First, draw a large oak tree on the flipchart paper, write the names 'Father', 'Son' and 'Holy Spirit' on the tree and place it in the centre of the group. As a group, consider what God's family tree looks like. At the baptism, the candidate will be baptised 'in the name of the Father, the Son and the Holy Spirit', and this activity gives an opportunity to explore what these names mean and how God can be three-in-one. Do not seek to explain the Trinity but rather rejoice in the wonder and diversity of God: it is not a problem to be solved but a wonder to be enjoyed. (The tree may not look like a normal family tree, with branches and marriages, but reference to the three interlocking circles on page 24 may be helpful.)

When the three names of the Trinity are there, it could be interesting to think about what other names may be in God's family tree. God has lots of other names; perhaps some of these could be introduced, to show how God is known by names that describe the things he has done and what he is like.

Split the group into twos or threes and hand each subgroup some of the cards from Appendix 6 (swap them around if you wish); these suggest Bible characters who can be added to God's family tree. They were ordinary people who came to know God and walked closely with God through their lives.

Look through the cards and discuss the following questions:

- What stands out to you about God's family?
- Are there any similarities between the stories?
- How many different names do you know for God?

Then let everyone choose where to place the cards on the family tree. Some discussion can be had about why they placed the cards where they did.

Provide some blank cards on which the group can fill in names of people they know who have been baptised, people who have a close relationship with God (these could be neighbours, friends, family members, or TV or film personalities), or people who have responded to God's calling in what they do or the way they live their lives.

Finally, ask each individual to write their own name on a blank card and place it on the tree. Discuss the following questions:

- Looking at the names you have placed on the tree, how many different communities do they belong to (for example, school, work, midweek group)?
- What does it mean to be a part of God's family?

If appropriate, encourage the group members to take a photo of the tree on their phones and save it as their screensaver.

Starters you can use with Option 1 main
- Here's my family
- My family tree
- What am I part of?
- Where am I in the community?

Desserts you can use with Option 1 main
- Prayers
- Poems
- Questions

Option 2:
God's community (family)

 Allow 20–30 minutes

You will need:
Copies of Appendix 7 cut into cards (the number of sets of copies will depend on whether you use this activity with more than one group); some additional blank cards (including a few on which you've written other activities specific to your church community); pens. NB: Instead of cards, you could use pictures or photographs

What goes on in the life of a church community? This activity enables us to consider what it is like to be part of the church. It may be that the candidates will see how they can be part of this church and join in as part of the family.

Mix up the cards, including a few blank cards on which people can write down their own suggestions. Then ask the group to sort the cards into the following areas:

- Things we might do together in an act of worship.
- Things we might do in our local community.
- Things we might do in our church community.
- Words that describe the way the people are in our church community.

In conversation while sorting the cards, draw out answers to the following questions:

- What does God's family look like?
- What sort of things do you do in your church community?

Some of the items on the list will also provide a way in to exploring why we do particular things. For example:

- 'Communion' may lead to an explanation of the exodus story and of the Last Supper.
- 'Praying' may be an opportunity to look at the Lord's Prayer, the Methodist Covenant Prayer or the Baptism Prayer.
- 'Caring' might be explored using the parable of the prodigal son or the parable of the sheep and the goats.

Once the cards have been sorted, explore the following questions:

- Are there any cards that surprise you?
- Is anything missing?
- What makes up a community?
- What makes up a family?

Consider where each of the above activities takes place. If the group or family are new to the church, a conversation could be had about how to get involved in the activities.

Starters you can use with Option 2 main
- Here's my family
- My family tree
- What am I part of?
- What families do

Desserts you can use with Option 2 main
- Prayers
- Poems
- Questions

Option 3:
What does it mean to belong?

 Allow 30 minutes

You will need:
Flipchart paper; felt-tip pens; maps of your church; maps of the local community

This activity can be done by individuals in groups. It explores what it means to belong to a community (to be a member, a part of the family of God).

Baptism is the initiation into the family of the church. It shows that you belong to the people of God. Consider how we experience this belonging. Some people may feel that they belong to the family before their baptism. (So what is it that began this process of belonging?) Others may feel as if they are coming in from the outside. (So what invitation was there, what open door, that encouraged them to come forward for this exciting service of baptism?)

Where there is mutual understanding, there is a feeling of belonging. When someone feels that they belong, there is an opportunity for commitment, participation, responsibility, resilience, positive management of conflict and consequent growth within the group. The feeling of belonging comes when those joining a group and those within it work towards mutual understanding. They do this by talking, questioning, clarifying, identifying, negotiating and setting common goals.

Split the group into threes (and twos, if necessary). Give each subgroup a flipchart page that has been divided into three sections (each section roughly the same size), felt-tip pens and copies of the maps.

Ask the subgroups to assign team roles (for example, timekeeper, spokesperson) and to allocate one section of the flipchart page to each person in the group.

Allow the subgroup members five minutes to draw all the places they feel they belong to. They may refer to the maps for ideas, if they wish. After five minutes, allow each person to share their drawings with their own subgroup.

Next, ask the nominated spokesperson from each subgroup to put the drawings together and present their subgroup's 'map of belonging' to the other groups. Allow brief explanations or additions to be made if necessary by the rest of the subgroup.

Ask everyone to turn over their pieces of flipchart paper. Allow them five minutes to draw a picture of a church and write round the outside what it might mean to belong to a church or church group. After five minutes, ask each person to share their work with their own subgroup.

Then, ask the nominated spokesperson from each subgroup to put the drawings together and present their subgroup's 'map of belonging to the church' to the other groups. Allow brief explanations or additions to be made if necessary by the rest of the subgroup.

During the discussions, try to address the following questions:

• Where do we feel we belong?
• What makes us feel that we belong?
• What makes us commit to a group or activity?
• What would it feel like to belong to a church?

Starters you can use with Option 3 main
- What am I part of?
- Where am I in the community?
- What families do

Desserts you can use with Option 3 main
- Prayers
- Poems
- Questions
- Invitations

Option 4:
When Jesus throws a party!  Allow 20–30 minutes

You will need:
(Depending on how you decide to deliver this activity) Pre-prepared members of your church community and any appropriate props (if you plan to dramatise the stories)

We are looking here at parties of biblical proportions. Explore the stories, focusing on the generosity, abundance, grace and wonder of the meals and parties where Jesus was present. Explain that we are preparing for another party that Jesus is hosting, the baptism. Take time to talk through the aspects of the baptism service and to explore these dynamics of wonder, mystery, generosity and abundance. Look forward to what will happen at the baptism service.

You may like to dramatise the Bible reading (perhaps with pre-prepared members of the church family and props).

Otherwise, you could use the following technique to explore the stories suggested:

- Ask the group to close their eyes, relax and listen to your voice.
- Ask the group to imagine themselves as one of the characters in the story (for example, the boy, Jesus, a disciple or a member of the crowd).

- What would they have seen, smelt and heard?
- How would they be feeling?
- What were their expectations of Jesus?
- Why had they come to hear him?
- What do they think Jesus' message was for them?

Bring out the following points as you explore each of the stories.

Jesus feeding the 5000 (John 6:1–13)

Tell the story of how Jesus asked his disciples to get food to feed all the people, and describe their response.

Explain how the small boy brought forward the little that he had. Describe how Jesus blessed the food and the disciples shared it out.

Marvel that there were actually more than 5000 people: that figure only counted the men (see Matthew 14:21). This was a big party! Consider how big a gathering it was, and ask, are that many coming to the baptism? How would you invite them all? What kind of things would you need to plan for that many people?

Stress that we are not looking for explanations of the miracle here, but focusing on the generosity of God. When Jesus throws a party, there is plenty for everyone and more besides. At the end of the feeding of the 5000, everyone had had their fill and there were twelve baskets of pieces left over. That's quite a party!

The wedding at Cana (John 2:1–10)

Tell the story, highlighting that we often focus on the miracle of water that becomes wine, but look at how much wine there was! There were 120–180 gallons of it. Wonder at the generosity and abundance we see when God throws a party.

The last supper (Mark 14:22–25)

Here, Jesus celebrates a special meal with his disciples, a meal that we have continued to share ever since that day.

This is a meal of simple fare. It does not have the same extravagance as in our first two examples, and yet it is full of great richness and wondrous generosity.

Zacchaeus (Luke 19:1–10)

This mysterious generosity, not seen just in abundance, is also present in many other meals that Jesus shared, such as the meal with Zacchaeus. We do not know what they ate, but the generosity is seen in the fact that Jesus chose to eat with him at all.

Jesus was always in trouble for eating with the people he chose to come to his parties—and now he chooses to throw a party at this baptism.

Sum up with the following questions:

- Think of how we will know about Jesus' presence at the baptism.
- Where will we see his generosity?
- Where will we spot his abundance?
- Who will we be surprised to see at the party?
- In what ways will it be mysterious and wonderful?

Starters you can use with Option 4 main
- What families do
- Party planning

Desserts you can use with Option 4 main
- Prayers
- Poems
- Questions
- Invitations

Option 5:
Organise a baptism rehearsal    Allow 30–40 minutes

You will need:
(Depending on how you decide to deliver this activity) Appropriate baptism symbols for your setting (such as water, oil, candle, service books); pre-prepared members of your church community; the baptism candidate and family

A wedding rehearsal is a normal part of the preparation for a marriage service. More churches seem to be having baptism rehearsals now, too, to prepare the family and candidates for what will take place at the service on the day of the baptism. Each person baptised follows on in a great line of millions from past times, from every nationality and in all parts of the world who have been baptised. They are part of a wonderful family spanning time and place.

A rehearsal is a perfect opportunity to walk through the service but also to explain what happens at each point and why it is done as it is. Make sure you don't only describe the mechanics of the service but also explore together the wonder and mystery of this great sacrament.

The rehearsal should be a time for the candidates and families to get comfortable in the church so that they know where they will be and what they will be doing, but it should also be a time when they can start to experience the wonder of baptism and look forward with anticipation to the big day.

If you choose not to have a full rehearsal, simply gather together all the elements that make up the baptism service and take some time to unpack what the symbols mean. Make water, oil, candles and service books available.

In the 'Enjoy the party!' section that follows, there are resources for looking at different elements of the baptism service. These may be used at the rehearsal in preparation for the day itself.

Starters you can use with Option 5 main
- My family tree
- Where am I in the community?
- What families do
- Party planning

Desserts you can use with Option 5 main
- Prayers
- Poems
- Questions
- Invitations

 Starters

Here's my family

 Allow 5–10 minutes

You will need:
Some family photos

In preparation for your meeting, ask those who will be there to bring along some family photos.

This is an ideal activity for a meeting that takes place in the candidate's home, as there are often family photos around the room. These can be used to open discussion about being part of a family.

Each person can introduce their family using the photos. Take time to listen carefully to each person as they introduce their family.

Enable the family to describe how the photographs show that the candidate is part of the family. It may be that they look like other members of the family, or that the photographs are taken at particular times (such as holidays or parties) or places.

My family tree

 Allow 10–15 minutes

You will need:
Pieces of paper; pens

Create a special family tree. This is not to be an exercise in genealogy but a fun activity to explore how we are part of a family group.

Ask the candidate to write their own name at the centre of a piece of paper. (Parents bringing infants for baptism should complete the activity for their child.) Now ask them to write the names of their direct family (blood relations). Some will be able to get further than others, but encourage people to create a good list of relations. They can put them anywhere on the paper they like to create an image of how they fit into their family.

Candidates may be as technical or creative as they wish. Some may place names randomly round the paper; others might place people in groups to show how close they are to each other. Some may place those they see every day close by and those they see rarely further away. Some may link people together with lines; others may draw bubbles or circles. Some may have complicated family lives that they can show too. It must be clear that this is not a judgmental exercise but an opportunity to celebrate being part of a family group.

Once the close family group is created, new groups can be added. What about pets, or people who are special, such as teachers or school friends? Older candidates may also like to add people who have been important to them in the past. The people on the tree may no longer be alive but they are still part of the candidate's special family.

By the end of this activity, the piece of paper should show the special family surrounding the candidate. This is the family of which they are part. It should be an encouraging picture. Each person should be able to celebrate the special relationships that support them.

What am I part of?

 **Allow 10 minutes**

You will need:
Pieces of paper; pens

This activity can be used as a basis to explore how we become members of the church in baptism and what our membership means to us. Be excited about how people are part of groups and part of communities. Show interest in exploring these groups and how the candidates are part of them. We are preparing the candidate to be part of the most wonderful community, the people of God.

First, write the name of the candidate at the centre of a piece of paper. Around it, write all the groups and organisations that the candidate is a part of. They might include family, uniformed organisations, school, postnatal class, local street, local community and the human race.

Try to be as open as possible, to allow as many groups as possible to be on the list. Some children and adults can be part of lots of groups, but others may not feel that they are part of any group. Aim to get as big a list as possible for each person.

If you are working with a group of baptism candidates, you could start to put the lists together, to see where they overlap. This could also be done if you are working with a family bringing an infant for baptism. Ask the parents to complete a list of the groups they are part of, too, and see where the overlaps occur within the family.

When the lists have been created, consider how the candidates know that they are part of these groups. How did they first join them? Was there a particular moment when their membership started? Did they belong to the group for a while before they joined officially? Do they have to wear anything to show that they are members of these groups? Are there rules that they have to follow or things they have to (or are supposed to) do because they are part of these groups? What are the groups for? Why do they exist and what difference do they make to the people in them and to those outside them?

Where am I in the community?  Allow 5–10 minutes

You will need:
Pieces of paper; pens

This is another paper activity, but with fewer words. Listen carefully to the answers each person gives about other places, and consider whether there are things we can learn about the church or ways in which it is different from other community activities.

Each person should draw a picture of the place where they live at the centre of the piece of paper. Then they should start to create a map of the places in the community where they go. These places may include school or work, the church, places where other family members live, shops and the local park. Encourage people to be creative in thinking about where they go and where they spend their time.

Take time then to think about who we meet in these places and what we do there. Are these places important to us and, if so, why? Are the places easy to reach or easy to get into? Are there rules about who can get in? How did we find out about them? Who else have we told about them?

Discuss the places where people in the community meet and the things that they do in the neighbourhood. What are the games they always play and the 'rituals' that always happen when people meet in these places?

All these answers can then be explored in relation to the church and what we do in this building.

If you are working with a larger group, it may be interesting to create the maps in small groups or as a whole group. This way, there may be discussions about where people meet up and a variety of input about each place on the map.

Another possibility would be to create a list of places that people go to, then ask each person to draw a picture or take a photo of that place and bring them all together to create a map in a collage style.

What families do

 **Allow 10 minutes**

No equipment is needed for this activity

This is a discussion activity, so no further items are needed. It opens up the opportunity to talk about becoming part of the church family, which is an important step in baptism.

Talk about family life. Ensure that you keep the discussion very open, as each person may have a very different experience of what a family is and what it is like to be part of one.

Talk together about what happens in families. What things do families do? For example, explore how each family eats: some may have a meal together; others may sit in front of the TV while they eat; others may all eat separately. Make no judgments about each family but enjoy the variety and encourage each person in what they say. Ask, 'Are there times when meals are different or special? When? How is a meal made special?'

Explore other things that families do, such as shopping and celebrating (think about Christmas and birthdays and other special celebration times). Talking may be another area to think about. Again, there will be a wide range of answers here, from families who talk lots and others who rarely meet. Encourage each person in what they offer to the discussion and be sensitive to everyone's input.

Perhaps you can introduce other things that families do, too, which are perhaps a little more abstract. Families create memories. Think together about what these memories might be, and how they are made and captured. Families also grow and shrink as people are born and die. Think together sensitively about how this happens, how the family marks these times and the difference they make to the family.

All these aspects of family life (and others that the group adds) can then be thought through in relation to the church family. There will certainly be many similarities and perhaps some differences, too. Think together about how the church is similar to or different from the families we are already part of.

NB: The experiences of each person's family life can be vastly different. It is a subject that should be handled with great care but can be richly rewarding in encouraging people and valuing them. Always make sure that everyone has the opportunity to speak about their experience, and do not force anyone to speak who would rather keep silent. When people offer their thoughts, the group will follow the lead that you model. Be encouraging and value each person and their contribution. If someone in the group suggests that another person's experience is less valid, this opinion needs to be corrected. There is a practical lesson here in how the people of the family of God can value and respect each other.

Party planning  **Allow 5–10 minutes**

You will need:
Pieces of paper (or flipchart, if this is a whole-group exercise); a selection of coloured pens

This activity explores the party idea as a lead-in to baptism. Parties can be great fun! The key element, to get people started, will be choosing the theme for the party and what the feel of the party will be. Once that is decided, the details should follow quite easily. Keep people focused on the task of creating the whole party feel, and on making everything fit the theme they have chosen. If you are in a larger group, it may be that people can work in small subgroups rather than on their own, or the activity could be done as a whole-group exercise.

Imagine you are throwing your dream party. It might be a birthday party or a Christmas party; it might be a summer special or a school class end-of-year party.

Think of a theme for your party, and how you will show the theme at the event. What will you use for decorations? What will there be to eat? What activities will there be? You could draw a plan of what the room will look like or create a running order of what will happen when.

Now think about the invitations. What will they say and what will they look like? You could create the invitations, and share with each other what you have tried to show in the way you have designed them. Finally, think about who you will invite, and why.

As you discuss your magnificent party, think about what you would be looking forward to most about it, and which bits of the party will be the most important. What will you do if you cannot afford all that you are planning? What would you leave out? What will be your own role at this party?

 Desserts

Prayer

 **Allow 5–10 minutes**

> **You will need:**
> Pieces of paper; pens

Teaching and encouraging people to pray is something that many of us should do more often. Preparation for a baptism is an ideal time to model prayer and to give people confidence to pray themselves. Whatever starter and main course you have selected, this is an ideal dessert activity!

- **Reflective prayer:** As your time together draws to a close, take time together to think over the things you have talked about. Perhaps people can be encouraged to think about their favourite or the most important things they have considered in the session. Then, have a time to be still and remember those favourite and important things.
- **More active prayer:** Active prayer is also important sometimes (prayer is not only about sitting quietly). You could start by having pieces of paper around the room, each of which summarises in a few words or with a few pictures the different topics covered in the evening, one piece of paper for each topic covered. It may be that creating these pieces of paper could be a reflective exercise done by the candidates. There can then be a time when people write on the paper what they enjoyed most about each activity. These pieces of paper can be collected together for a gathering prayer of thanksgiving.
- **Thanksgiving prayer:** It would be good for someone to model a prayer to give thanks for everything that people have said or written down, and to pray for the candidates as they are getting ready for baptism. The prayer should be simple and a good model of how prayer can be said, such as the Lord's Prayer.
- **DIY prayer:** Candidates could be encouraged to create their own prayer. It could be either a prayer for them to say each day up to their baptism or something to be said in public at the baptism service.
- **Private prayer:** People should not have to share their prayers if they wish them to be private, but please make sure that you give them an opportunity to seek your advice and encouragement.

Poems

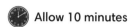 **Allow 10 minutes**

You will need:
Pieces of paper; pens; sticky notes

In a similar way to the prayer activity above, this could be an opportunity to create something for use at the baptism service itself. Remember, though, that writing poems can be a difficult and daunting prospect for those who find words difficult.

- **Reflective poems:** Take time together to think through the themes you have covered as a group. You might want to talk about belonging, about God's love, or about being part of the family of the church. Whatever the topic has been, think through some of the important aspects that have emerged. Find some good words to describe what you have talked about. These words can then form the basis of some poems. People can add in lots of their own words if they choose, but it is sometimes easier to have done some creative thinking together first, to get started.
- **Kennings:** It is possible to write poems together using 'kennings', which are two-word phrases that describe what things do. For example, a key is a 'door opener' and a candle could be a 'light giver'. Think about some of the topics and issues you have talked about, and think of some words to describe them, using this technique. If you have been talking about families, think of kennings for what families do or what they are like or what it feels like to belong to a family. If you have talked about parties that Jesus hosted, think of words to describe things in the story, such as the bread and wine, what the crowd of 5000 people was like, and so on. If you have had a rehearsal in the church, think of kennings for the different items used in the service and the different parts of the church where the service will take place. I wonder what a good kenning for a godparent might be, or for the candidate, or for the minister!

     Write each kenning down on a sticky note and gather the notes together, sticking them on a wall or a large piece of paper. Then read them out as a poem. These poems can often be very moving and descriptive and are amazingly simple to create, once people understand the concept.

Questions

 **Allow 5-10 minutes**

> **You will need:**
> A6 cards; pens

With the right encouragement, candidates, parents and families, and especially children, can often ask some very perceptive questions. Sometimes, challenging people to think of particularly tricky questions can be a good way to set up the opportunity to think them through. If the candidates are happy to write questions for the congregation to answer, this would be a wonderful way to explore baptism and faith with the church family. What better way to excite a congregation about a baptism the following week than to challenge them with some of the questions from the candidates?

Give each person two A6 cards and ask them to think about what they have done in the time you have spent together, the baptism service, or anything to do with the church, baptism, faith, God, and so on. Ask them to write down two questions and then gather the cards together in a box.

Pull out cards at random and consider what the answers might be. Don't feel that you have to be the fount of all knowledge. Saying that you don't know the answer is a good answer, if it is the truth!

Take the opportunity to open questions up to the group itself. It may be that some of the candidates have the best answers to other people's questions. Encourage people to talk and learn together as they try to answer the questions.

Invitations

 **Allow 5-10 minutes**

> **You will need:**
> Blank pieces of paper or A6 card; coloured pens; access to a colour photocopier and laminator, if available (optional)

This activity could be an opportunity to create something for use at the baptism service itself.

Think together about the main themes of the baptism service. What are the important things that are going to happen? What are you most looking forward to? How will the church look and feel on the day?

Then create invitations that capture these characteristics of your baptism service. Think about colours to reflect the feeling of baptism (children may wish to refer to the colour wheel in the *My Baptism Journey* activity book). Think of pictures and words to describe what is going to happen, and think of the right words of invitation for the people who will be invited.

If you have the capacity, it may be possible to reproduce the invitations so that the candidates can give them out to the members of their family who are going to be at the service.

If you are unable to reproduce the invitations, it may be more appropriate to create a different type: decide together what might be important to God about baptism, and then create an invitation to the candidate from God. A further twist could be to create invitations from God to each other, and swap them so each candidate has an invitation created by someone else with a special message inside.

When all the preparation is done, it is time to look forward to the day itself.

✢

Enjoy the party!

Session aim

To explore the themes of baptism itself—its symbolism, its mystery and meaning, and its celebration.

Setting the scene

When the time for preparation is done, it is time to look forward to the party itself. The service of baptism is a once-in-a-lifetime moment, and it will be a day of celebration and thanksgiving. It should indeed have the feel of a party. The party will be starting in heaven among the angels and it is important that we capture the celebration in the service too.

There are many themes that we can bring out in the service, giving plenty of opportunity for variety in the many baptisms performed at your church.

The first theme is baptism itself. This celebration is something that many people in our churches have experienced themselves. The celebration of a new baptism gives the chance to reflect on our own baptism and to be encouraged in what it means for us and for those who come to our churches for baptism. On each occasion, we should be able to wonder anew at the magnificent miracle of baptism, that in this sacrament we are made new in our response to the amazing love of God. Baptisms can be a time to re-excite those who have been through this experience and set those who have not been baptised thinking about whether it is something they could consider.

There is also an opportunity to explore what baptism is. The service of baptism is full of symbolism. We can use oil to reflect holiness and the way God receives us into his family. During the service, the sign of the cross is made on the forehead of the candidate. This basic Christian sign marks us with the symbol of Christ's death and the means of our salvation. We receive the sign of Christ. We use water, showing how we are made clean, how we are refreshed, and how we pass through death from our old life and into the new life of Christ. We can use candles to show how we pass from darkness into light and how we shine with a new light, the light of Christ.

The symbols themselves give plenty of opportunity to experience the mystery of the service, and the truths of which they speak give further cause to wonder at the miracle of baptism. They are a way in to exploring themes of forgiveness, holiness, creation, death and resurrection, thanksgiving, faith, hope, love and myriad other characteristics of the God in whose name we are baptised.

The theme of celebration must also be at the forefront of our service. If we do not celebrate a baptism, then we are not aware of its significance. There is plenty to draw from the theme of celebration. The joy of God and the heavenly host at the addition of a new member to the family of God is one strand. The turning to new life and the declaration of following Christ are other causes for thanksgiving.

This theme often sits easily with those coming for baptism, too. A family bringing their child may have arranged a family party. There may be many people at the church who only meet up at baptisms, weddings and funerals. We should not underestimate the significance of this day for the family, and we should seek to enable them to recognise in the midst of this special social celebration that there is an even greater party going on—a party celebrating the love of God for us.

This theme of celebration and party is something not only for the family to build on; it is also for the church to think about. Some churches may have only a few baptisms each year, and it may be possible to invest time and energy in emphasising this day of celebration. The church building can be decorated, with flower arrangements, focal displays and banners adding to the sense of celebration in the church, just as party decorations would add to the sense of celebration at a birthday party. This service is a celebration of a new birth, the start of a new life in Christ, and we should mark it appropriately.

Even if there are many baptisms in a church, we should not become numb to the sense of celebration or lazy in the way we use the surroundings and the setting. Decorations and focal displays about baptism are suitable to have around the church even when there is not a baptism: we are the baptised people of God. In many traditional churches, there will be a stained-glass window showing the baptism of Jesus. This is a means by which people can learn and remember the wonder of baptism every time they are in church. The window is not covered up when a baptism is not happening, so a display about baptism or decorations to celebrate baptism would not be out of place in weeks when such a service was not taking place either.

At a baptism, the setting and the symbols speak of our experience of God and the love that he shows to us. It is a party to which he calls us to come and celebrate, and at this party there are people who have particular roles to play.

The candidate is sometimes seen as the focus of the day. They may be a babe in arms, a toddler, a child, a teenager, or an adult of more mature years. Whoever they are, this day is their time to declare their response to God and the beginning of a new stage in their spiritual life. Taking this as a theme within the service provides teaching not only for the candidate but also for their supporters and family and for all those who have been, or might like to be, baptised.

For younger candidates, there will also be parents and godparents who fulfil key roles on the day. They will declare their faith in God on behalf of the child and will promise to bring the child up in the way and the teaching of the faith they declare. There is plenty of opportunity here to explore what the promises mean and how we might live them out. It is important that we take what may seem abstract and create a clear vision of its application in real life. Again, there may be people in the congregation, perhaps not godparents on the day, who are already godparents to other children or who may be asked to be godparents in the future. Looking at this role in a baptism service should encourage and inspire them in their calling.

The family of the candidate is also important in the service. While the god-parents have a specific duty of care, the family and their support of the candidate will make a big difference in the future. Looking at this theme of support and encouragement from the wider family can strengthen the confidence of the person being baptised. Especially with older candidates, it may be useful to highlight their journey to baptism and their desire for what it will mean in their future.

The family of the church also has an important role to play in the baptism service. The church family makes promises too, to welcome the newly baptised person and support them in their faith. This is a promise in which we are often found wanting. Much work could be done in church before and during baptisms, looking at the church's responsibility in welcoming people who come to baptism and ensuring that they are encouraged to become full members of the church family.

All these different groups of people at the baptism are important, but it should never be forgotten that the most important presence at the party is God. Baptism is given in the name of the Father, Son and Holy Spirit. There is every opportunity to explore the wonder of the God whom we experience as Creator, Redeemer and Strengthener. In baptism we encounter God in a special way, and this service is a gift for exploring the wonder of the God we believe in. Do not miss the chance to be excited about God!

Baptism is a moment of new beginning. For some families and churches, the baptism service is the end to which they are working. There is a feeling that when the service is done and the day is over, the job is complete. Baptism, though, is the start of something, a door through which we pass into a new stage of life. Themes can be developed in the service to highlight this life ahead. Looking at hopes and dreams for the new future, exploring how the promises made can be lived out, and thinking about how life may or may not be different after baptism are all possibilities for developing this theme.

The permanence of the invisible badge of baptism that we wear is another area of opportunity here. Names have permanence for us. Baptism is no longer the moment at which we receive our names, but the names are used as a crucial part of the baptism service. Using the name as a hook on which to develop a theme at the baptism service can provide a reminder of baptism well beyond the limits of the day itself.

The wonder of baptism means that lots of themes can be developed at the service. If we are as amazed and excited by a baptism as we ought to be, then the difficulty is really in what to leave out rather than what to put in. Do not feel the need to explain everything. Sometimes symbolism is best in its symbolic form, rather than being 'reduced to an explanation'. Do not feel that you can never use the same material twice: we often enjoy a favourite meal again and again, even with simple foods. Baptism is a party, and parties can often be places where we anticipate our favourite party foods.

The main charge to all of us who find ourselves in key roles at baptism is to remember and revel in the wonder of the mystery that takes place there. In baptism, we respond to the wonderful love of God and turn to him at a moment in time that will be with us for the rest of our lives. If we remember this basic and amazing fact, then baptism can only be a celebration, and our service should capture that at its heart.

Session activities

The activities below can be used in a variety of settings. They can be developed in the baptism service itself; they might be used before the service, to enable families and candidates to engage with the service more on the day; they might be used by those working with children and young people when talking about baptism; or they could be used by the whole church in all-age worship, to explore the theme of baptism. They are here to provide seeds that could be grown into a harvest of opportunities to explore and be excited about baptism.

 Main course

Option 1: Water

Allow 20–30 minutes

> **You will need:**
> (Depending on what you choose to do) Water in vessels; pens; paper; pictures of 'watery' Bible stories; equipment to make a banner or display

At the simplest of baptism services, water is used. It is one of the crucial elements and symbols of baptism. Here are some suggestions for the baptism service:

- **Watery words:** Get some water and explore what it is like. We so often take water for granted and fail to truly notice it. Examine carefully what it looks like, how it moves, and how we can change its appearance when we move it around. See how it becomes agitated and how it calms down. Create a list of words to describe what water is like (not just 'wet'!).

- **Water use:** Create a list of the ways in which we use water. Perhaps you can try some of them out in the group. In particular, 'to refresh' and 'to clean' are two uses that could be explored further. In baptism, we see the way that water refreshes us, giving us new life; we also see how water cleans us. (Mention that in baptism, we are washed not just on the outside but also on the inside, making us fully clean.)

- **Bible stories:** Look at some Bible stories about water. In many baptism services, there will be some Bible stories mentioned in the service itself. They might include the story of creation, where God's Spirit moved over the face of the waters; the story of the people of Israel leaving slavery and going to freedom when God parted the waters of the Red Sea; and the story of the baptism of Jesus (this might be referred to in the prayer over the water before baptism). Look at these stories together in a Bible or using some pictures. It may be that you have a stained-glass window in your church that shows one or more of these events. Explore how water is used in the stories and discuss how they reflect what happens at the baptism service in church today.

- **Create a banner or a display:** As well as being a crucial part of baptism, water is key to our survival. We are made mostly of water, and we need it to survive. If we were not able to find water, we would not live for many days. It is crucial to life and crucial in baptism. This theme could be explored by creating a banner or a display. Gather material about water and make a display to show how we use water in our lives, and how we use it in baptism too. In the display, explore what water reminds us of in baptism and why it is important in the service.

Starters you can use with Option 1 main
- Questions
- Feely box
- Baptism words

Desserts you can use with Option 1 main
- The service
- Hopes and dreams

Option 2: Light

 **Allow 20–30 minutes**

You will need:
(Depending on what you choose to do) Different sources of light; candles and matches; special baptism candles; equipment to make a banner or display

Picking up the way water is explored in Option 1, the same sort of activities can be done with light. Lighting a candle is often the final act of the baptism service. Here are some ideas.

- **Sources of light:** There are lots of different kinds of light: sunlight, light from a lightbulb, light that comes from a TV or a digital game, LED lights and lights in phones and watches. Look around your church or room to see how many different light sources you can find. Explore what 'Jesus is the light of the world' might mean.
- **Candlelight:** In baptism we use a candle, which is a particular form of light. Think of how we use candles now, and how special they can be to us. Now that we have electric light, we use candles for special moments, rather than all the time. Look at candlelight and see how it is different from other light. Look at what is good about it. See how candlelight is a living light: it is not still but

it moves around. It is also fragile and can be dangerous. Obviously, care needs to be taken, especially when working with children. Your church's health and safety regulations should be followed at all times, but these precautions are worth taking: now that we use candles in our homes so rarely, there is a magical quality about them. Services such as Christingle, when children are able to hold candles and the church is lit by candlelight alone, can be spectacular events and very memorable. Take care, and enjoy exploring candlelight!

- **Light in the darkness:** Think about how light and darkness are different. Why is being in the dark so difficult? How can even a small light in darkness make a difference? Think together about why we use a candle in the baptism service, and what it means to the person who receives it. Talk about how, at baptism, we pass from darkness into light and how we shine with a new light, the light of Christ. Making a display or creating a banner about darkness and light can be a wonderful way of exploring this aspect of baptism.

- **Baptism candles:** Look together at the baptism candles used in your church. They may have designs on them to show that they have been made especially for baptisms. Your group could design baptism candles too, to show why light is important in baptism.

Starters you can use with Option 2 main

- Questions
- Feely box
- Baptism words

Desserts you can use with Option 2 main

- The service
- Hopes and dreams
- Godparent letter

Option 3: Oil

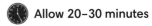 Allow 20–30 minutes

> **You will need:**
> (Depending on what you choose to do) Different types of oil; special baptism oil; paper; pens

Not all churches use oil in baptism, and it is not a requirement of the service. However, if your tradition and practice does include oil, it is worth taking the opportunity to explore it and its use in the service. Here are some suggestions:

- **Oil research:** Look at the oil and smell it. Oil is a wonderful thing to find out about because it is so unusual. The oil used in churches will usually have been blessed by a bishop on a service that takes place only on Maundy Thursday. This in itself can make it appear a mysterious and intriguing product. The smell of the oil also enables us to use our senses to explore it, and the aroma can be quite pungent. There are three types of oil that many churches hold. Discuss how they are different, and find out what each of them is used for. Find out where the minister gets the church oil from and consider why it is special, not like the oil we buy in the supermarket or at the garage.
- **Anointing oil:** Find some places in the Bible where oil is mentioned. A word search on a Bible website or a concordance will bring up many references, including Psalm 133, which describes oil poured over Aaron's head and running down his beard. This comes from the story about when he was chosen to serve God, and reflects the way we become part of God's people in baptism. Psalm 23 also contains a reference to oil: 'You anoint my head with oil'. Again, this is about being recognised as one of God's people and being cared for by God himself. There are wonderful connections to be made here with baptism, which you could explore together.
- **Burial oil:** In the Gospels, we read about Jesus having oil poured on his feet. He describes this as being a preparation for his burial (John 12:3–7). In baptism, we speak of being baptised into Jesus' death and into his resurrection. Again, the oil can be a way in to exploring this aspect of baptism.
- **Oil uses:** Oil is not something we seem to use much in our homes now. We do use oil for cooking, but in former times it was an essential everyday item; it was used for preserving, lighting, cleaning and many other regular tasks. Make a list together of all the past and present uses of oil you can think of.

Starters you can use with Option 3 main
- Questions
- Feely box
- Baptism words
- Invisible ink

Desserts you can use with Option 3 main
- The service
- Hopes and dreams

Option 4: Crosses

 Allow 20–30 minutes

You may need:
A selection of crosses

The cross is the symbol of the church. In this age, it may be seen as the 'logo' of our faith. At baptism, the symbol of the cross is one of the requirements of baptism. Sometimes it is made with the oil and sometimes it is drawn invisibly with the finger or with the water of baptism. However it is drawn, usually on the forehead of the candidate being baptised, this is the mark of Christ, the symbol of his death and the means of forgiveness and salvation.

Take time to explore your church and see how many crosses you can find. There may be crosses around the worship area that are easy to find. There may be crosses in stained-glass windows. Look more closely to find others that are not so easy to see. There might be crosses on some of the books or on items on the church noticeboard. There may be crosses that some of the people present are wearing. Sometimes there are crosses in the designs of doors or windows. Once you start to notice crosses, you will find them everywhere. Children are especially good at finding those that adults miss. Look at the similarities and differences in the crosses you have seen.

When you have found as many as you can, take time to think about why the cross is so important in a church. Tell the story of how Jesus was crucified, nailed to a cross until he was dead. It was a very sad thing, but it was a wonderful thing too. Explain that Jesus rose again after three days and became alive to show us that death is not the final end that it seems to be. Nothing can separate us from God, not even death.

It may be appropriate to encourage people to make the sign of the cross on their own forehead and think of what it means to have that sign, like an invisible badge. In a baptism service, this signing will be done by the minister, but it may also be good to ask other members of the baptism party, such as parents, godparents and sponsors, to make the sign on the candidate's forehead.

Starters you can use with Option 4 main
- Questions
- Feely box
- Baptism words
- Logo game
- Invisible ink

Desserts you can use with Option 4 main
- The service
- Hopes and dreams
- Godparent letter

Option 5: Baptism symbols Allow 20–30 minutes

You will need:
A selection of baptism symbols (water, light, oil, cross and so on)

If you are using this material in a family service looking at baptism, or in a meeting where you are preparing for a baptism service, it may be possible to split your group into four smaller groups, or into many smaller groups.

Give each group one of the four symbols considered in the four earlier options—water, light, oil and cross. Each group should then work on a different symbol. If you have lots of groups, several of them may be exploring each topic.

Allow the groups 15 minutes to try to find out as much as they can about each symbol, possibly using the options above as a guide.

When they have had some time to find out about their symbol, the whole group can come back together. The information that the smaller groups have discovered can be shared with everyone, focusing especially on why they think the symbol is important at a baptism.

It may be useful to have group leaders who can provide some structure to the symbol search. The options on the four separate symbols will be useful in giving guidance to the group leaders.

Starters you can use with Option 5 main
- Questions
- Feely box
- Baptism words
- Logo game
- Invisible ink

Desserts you can use with Option 5 main
- The service
- Hopes and dreams

Option 6: Who's who?

 Allow 20–30 minutes

You will need:
The baptism party

There is usually a cast of people present at a baptism, and it is useful to explore why they are there and what their role is to be at the service. If this is to be done during the service itself, it will be useful to ask those who are in the appropriate roles to step forward. If they feel confident enough, they may even be able to explain what they think is the best thing about being in their role that day. They may also be able to explain what they feel is the most important part of that role.

NB: When asking people questions in public, try not to put them on the spot. Tell them beforehand that you will ask them some questions, and ensure they are happy to be asked. Make sure, too, that you are gentle and encouraging. Give people an opportunity to think about the answers they might give to the questions you will ask. If they would rather not answer the questions in public, do not force them. This activity can be done as a whole church, thinking about how each person *might* feel.

It is good for the minister to explain their own role first, setting a model for the kind of answers people might give. Keep the answers as simple and uncomplicated as possible. Try not to be too deep, but seek to capture the wonder and joy of baptising people into the love of God and being part of such an important celebration.

Look at the role of the person being baptised. If they are too small to be able to respond for themselves, other people in the congregation might be able to suggest what they are thinking about the service and about being baptised. Again, try to capture the wonder and joy of the occasion. Highlight that this is a once-in-a-lifetime day, and often a family day, both for their own family and for the family of the church.

Ask the parents about their feelings on this special day. It may be appropriate to ask why they chose to bring their child for baptism and what it means to them.

Godparents have a very important and unusual role at a baptism. Think about how parents choose the people who will act as godparents, and what they will do at the service and after the service.

Ask the candidate's wider family about why they have come and what is so good about being at the service.

The church family members, too, have a role to play at the baptism. They are the family into which the candidate is being baptised, and they have a role of welcoming, nurturing and supporting this new member. Ask them how they will do that and what is so good about it.

Finally, do not forget that God is present at the baptism. Think together about what God thinks about the baptism. What do you think God's favourite bit might be, and what might God feel is the most important thing about the baptism service?

Starters you can use with Option 6 main
- Questions
- Baptism words
- John says
- Celebrations

Desserts you can use with Option 6 main
- Hopes and dreams
- Godparent letter
- Biography
- The service

Option 7: Baptism promises

 Allow 20–30 minutes

You will need:
The baptism party; a list of the promises made by the candidate and baptism party

This activity not only enables those making the promises to understand them better, but is also a reminder to all those who have been baptised of the promises that they should be trying to live by. This is an informative and very challenging activity.

A central part of the baptism service is the promises that are made by or on behalf of the candidate. The promises can sometimes be in a language that is very different from the words we normally use. Consider the promises together. Do not feel that you need to explain them; rather, try to explore what they mean.

Think about other ways of asking the same questions. What is it that each question is trying to find out? Why is the question being asked at a baptism? Think of ways in which the person answering the question could show their answer rather than speaking it. What sort of things will they do to show that they meant what they promised?

NB: Don't do this activity in a mastermind style, with each person being interrogated about the promises they will be making. Rather, enjoy the activity as a whole-church opportunity to look at the promises.

Starters you can use with Option 7 main
- Questions
- Baptism words
- John says

Desserts you can use with Option 7 main
- Godparent letter
- The service

Option 8:
What happens in baptism?

 Allow 20–30 minutes

You will need:
The baptism symbols; water; a doll

This activity is an excellent preparation for a family where there are children who are old enough to answer for themselves. It is also perfect for preparing a family at a rehearsal before the baptism, to show them what will happen on the day. The activity could easily be used on the day of the baptism itself as a sermon slot. If there are children being baptised who are not babes in arms but can engage with the doll, this can be a very visual way to explore what is going to happen to them in the service. It brings to life the symbolism and explains it not only to the children but, through the children's wonder, to the adults too.

Explore together what happens at a baptism service. Demonstrate what happens at the baptism service by 'baptising' a doll. People could be asked to help choose a name for the doll, and the different elements of the service can be demonstrated. The making of promises, the saying of prayers for the doll, the oil, the sign of the cross, the water and the lighted candle could all be parts of this demonstration.

Afterwards, there can be an opportunity for people to ask questions or to think about which bit of the real baptism service they are most looking forward to, why the different parts of the service are important and what they might show about the love of God.

If there are members of your group who are artistic, it may be possible to create a storyboard showing what happens at a baptism and describing the parts of a baptism service. Making the storyboard enables people to think about the different parts of the service, and it creates space to think about why those parts are important and what they signify.

Starters you can use with Option 8 main
- Questions
- Baptism words
- Celebrations
- Logo game
- Invisible ink

Desserts you can use with Option 8 main
- The service
- Hopes and dreams

Option 9: Welcome cards

 Allow 20–30 minutes

You will need:
Card; art materials

Even in its simplest form, this is a great activity. It encourages people to welcome the newly baptised person and encourages the person being baptised to feel very much part of the community. It also gives people an opportunity to think about why baptism is important and to capture the sense of celebration.

The activity can be done without any great preparation. As long as there are card, art materials and a place to work, it can be done individually in pews, in a corner of the church or in the Sunday school room, if you are lucky enough to have one.

Provide card and art materials and ask the group to create welcome cards for the person who is being baptised.

To add a twist to the activity, consider some further suggestions. For example, ask people, especially adults, to write a greeting that describes why being baptised is so important to them, or why they think it is so good to be baptised. You could ask that the cards particularly show how a baptised person becomes a member of the church or sees the love of God in a special way.

Try to enable people to explore baptism as they create their cards and messages, and you will also be ensuring that the messages created will add to the opportunity the candidates have to think further about what baptism means.

This simple activity can be done in many different ways. It is perfect for the congregation to undertake in the week before a baptism. If you have a children's activity time, it could be done then, producing cards for those to be baptised at the church. Groups linked to the church, including uniformed organisations and toddler groups, could also be encouraged to create cards. Adults could be given A6 pieces of card and asked to write short messages on them, which could be tied together with a ribbon to make a personal book of welcome.

The family of the candidate can also be involved in this activity. If you give the parents or the candidate a small pile of cards, they could give them out before the baptism or even on the day, asking people to write down what they most remember about the day and why it is so important. These cards may be gathered and kept as a a reminder of why the day was so important.

Starters you can use with Option 9 main
- Celebrations
- Invisible ink

Desserts you can use with Option 9 main
- Hopes and dreams
- Godparent letter
- Biography

 Starters

Questions  **Allow 10 minutes**

You may need:
Pieces of paper; pens; lists of unanswered questions from the group

It is always important to give people time to ask questions, and to take time to answer them carefully. Sometimes people are unable to listen to input because there are questions that they want answered first.

Ask people if they have any questions, and encourage them to ask them. Make sure that you give people time to think about questions they might wish to ask. There may be questions that have been left over from a previous time together, or questions that have occurred to people between your last meeting and the current one.

If your group did the 'Questions' activity as the 'Desserts' part of Session 1 (see page 49), you may already have some questions that candidates and their family have asked, for the congregation to answer during a church service. Read the questions before the service, check that there are not too many, and check that you are able to explore them usefully within the context of the service.

When it comes to answering the questions, do not feel that there has to be only one person answering or that everyone must be listening to an 'expert'. Rather, enjoy wondering together as a congregation about what the answers might be. Ask if anyone has any thoughts as to how to start to answer the questions. You will find much more interesting answers by thinking through them together than by reeling off a set answer. It may even be that the 'expert' learns something!

This dynamic of exploring things together is an exciting way of looking at issues in a church setting. For many years, our traditions have held to the view that the answers have to come from the front, but enabling a congregation to wonder together allows other people to explore in a much more engaging way the subjects that come up in church. It may be a greater challenge and encouragement to faith than any sermon or address.

Deal with responses sensitively. To begin with, people may feel very nervous. However, with greater experience and trust in the person asking them for a response, they will soon start to become more confident. Key elements for building that trust are that people are never pushed to give great supplementary answers to their initial response, and that their words will be accepted rather than judged. Their contribution needs to be valued if they are to feel they can respond again.

Be brave! This can feel like a very dangerous way to work, as you can never be sure what people will say, but experience shows that it can be very engaging and can help people to grow in their faith.

Feely box

 **Allow 10 minutes**

You will need:

A large cardboard box; scissors; various baptism-related objects to put inside the box (for example, a bowl of water, a shell, an unlit baptism candle, some oil, a cross)

Before the session, find a large cardboard box and cut two holes in the top, large enough for someone to put their arms through, but without seeing what is inside. (If you do not have a cardboard box, a large bag which you can put objects inside will work just as well.)

Inside the box, put a selection of objects. The 'contestants' should be able to guess what these objects are by touch alone. Any objects could be put inside, but connecting them to the baptism service will enable the game to become a way into one of the main activities or into further discussion about baptism or the baptism service.

At the session, ask for a brave volunteer to be your first contestant. Ask them to put their arms into the holes in the box and try to identify one of the objects by touch alone.

> The shell is another symbol that can be used at baptism. It has a practical use in that it is often used to scoop the water from the font to pour over the candidate's head. It has a deeper meaning, too, in that it is the symbol of a pilgrim.
>
> The shell is part of the shield that represents St James, and those who travelled to his shrine in Spain would often wear a shell on their hat to show that they were pilgrims on this special journey. The shell, then, has become a symbol of pilgrimage. It highlights that baptism is not only about the day of the baptism service, but is also about a lifetime journey of discipleship.

Baptism words

 **Allow 10 minutes**

You will need:
Pieces of paper/flipchart; pens

This is a game like the classic 'Hangman', although it is more helpful to create a baptism-linked image than the traditional gallows. A simple font shape or a church should enable a 'score' of incorrect guesses to be kept and create the challenge of completing the word before the number of guesses is up.

Show people the number of letters in the word and ask them to choose a letter of the alphabet. This could be done by inviting a single volunteer to the front, or by taking 'bids' from the congregation.

The words you choose to ask people to guess can lead into the topic of your 'main course' on baptism. You might choose words such as church, baptism, God, water, shell, oil, candle, light, promise, disciple, family, and so on. Make sure that you have a good mixture of easy words with some trickier ones (for example, symbolism, sacrament or pilgrimage) to test the adults too.

Either of the two images below could be used as the scoring system. The church can be drawn using just ten lines and the font using twelve, and will give people a chance to guess the words but feel the pressure of seeing the drawing grow as their guesses run out.

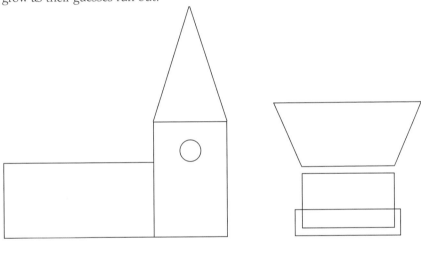

John says

 **Allow 10 minutes**

No equipment is needed for this activity

This is a variation on the game 'Simon says' and can be used as a way in to talking about God's call to us. 'John says' can be used to introduce the story of John the Baptist and the story of Jesus' baptism. It can also lead into thinking about our response to God's call, the promises of baptism and how we might try to live them out beyond the date of the baptism service.

Explain that you are going to give people instructions, but they must obey the instructions only if they are preceded by the words 'John says'.

You may say, 'John says, put your hands on your head' and you will expect people to follow your lead. 'John says, put your finger on your nose' should also get a positive response, but 'Put your right hand in the air' is not a command to be followed, as it is not preceded by the prescribed words.

Although this is traditionally a game for children, encourage everyone to join in. Enjoy sensitively the difficulties that the adults have. Use the following techniques to increase the suspense: choose a variety of fun actions; vary the speed with which you give instructions; play with silence, anticipation and runs of three or four instructions in a row. Enjoy the game!

Celebrations

 Allow 10 minutes

You will need:
Pieces of paper; pens

This activity introduces the theme of the baptism celebration.

Think together about celebrations. Make a list of celebrations that people have been to—for example, birthday parties, Christmas celebrations, and other celebrations such as school leaving parties or Valentine's Day parties. Try to gather a long list, and be interested in the answers people give. When you receive an answer, find out what kind of activities happened at the celebration and if it was a good celebration.

When you have completed the list, look more closely at what made these events a celebration. Are there some common themes that show what makes an event celebratory? Find out who went to the celebrations, and who chose the list of people to be invited. Find out too if there were any traditions that always happened at these events, such as singing 'Happy Birthday' or having a cake with candles.

Explore how celebrations are an important part of our lives: they mark special moments. It is good to mark special times and to share the times when others celebrate too. Think carefully about how your church celebrates baptism. Is it a celebration or is it difficult to see how it is different from a normal service ? How will people know that this is an event to celebrate?

Logo game

 **Allow 10 minutes**

You will need:
A selection of common logos (from labels on household products, and so on); pieces of paper; pens

This activity could be used to introduce the baptism theme of the 'invisible badge of the cross' and belonging to God's family.

Discuss how logos and symbols are all around us—road traffic signs that tell us what to do on the road, symbols on clothes telling us how they can be washed, and logos that show us which company makes a product or works in a particular building. Logos are there to say in pictures something that would take many words. They are easily recognisable and should tell us something about the company or 'brand' that they stand for.

Create a logo quiz. Show some logos and ask people to say where they come from or what they mean. Include some that are easy and some that might be a little more difficult.

When the logos have been identified, you could explore which are good logos and what makes them good. Is it that they are pleasant or memorable, or that they explain something about what they represent?

Perhaps you could think about some church logos. If your church has a logo of its own, you could include that too. As a group, think about logos that could be used for the church.

If appropriate, you may have time and opportunity for people to create some church logos or a baptism logo.

Invisible ink

 **Allow 10 minutes**

You will need:
Paper; pens

This is a simple game but it is a great way to bring and hold a group together. It is also a very easy way in which to highlight our roles in baptism, the act of faith in baptism, the invisible badge of the cross and the mystery of the miracle of baptism, which is something that changes us in a way we cannot see.

Say that people sometimes have handwriting that is difficult to read, but how about trying to read what someone is writing when they do not have a pen or pencil?

Ask someone to write a simple word such as 'house' with a pen on paper, so that everyone can see it. They should write it a letter at a time, and after each letter the congregation should try to guess what the word will be. Try this a few times so that people get the idea.

Now make it more difficult by asking the person to write a word not with a pen on paper, but in the air with their finger. It is not an easy thing to do. You could make this activity a little easier by choosing words that all have something to do with baptism.

When people become successful at working out the words, ask how they are managing to read what they cannot see. Explore how we can recognise things that are not necessarily visible.

People may be able to recognise the words in ways that can be useful when exploring themes around baptism. For example, some people may say that they watch very carefully, so that they can notice what the person is writing. Some may say that they imagine that the person is writing with a pen, and that they remember where the finger has just been, seeing in their mind the letter that has been written. Others may try to think about the whole word and anticipate what it might be by looking for a few particular letters, even if they cannot understand all of them.

 Desserts

Hopes and dreams
 **Allow 10 minutes**

You may need:
Pieces of paper; pens; A6 blank cards; hole punch; special ribbon

This activity allows the baptism party to create a special message for the candidate on the day of the baptism, which they will be able to keep as a memento and read in future years.

Before the service, ask members of the candidate's family to write down some of their hopes and dreams for the candidate's future. If the candidate is a babe in arms, it is a wonderful thing to ask the parents and godparents to do. If the candidate is older, it may be good to include their friends and wider family too.

Discuss how baptism is a special time of life: it is a time for looking to the future and recognising and praying for all that lies ahead. If appropriate, say that it has been wonderful to hear godparents and parents speak about their hopes for the future of their child and/or godchild. Explain that their 'Hopes and dreams' message does not need to be long, and it does not need to be read out; it could be kept safe until the child is old enough to be able to read it.

The activity does not need to be restricted to parents and godparents. You could give a small pile of A6 cards to the family, so that they can ask as many of the people at the baptism as they wish to write something. The cards can then have holes punched in them and be joined by a ribbon. This will make a very special baptism memento for the candidate.

Do not feel that this activity has to be for family only. Asking church family members to write their hopes and dreams for the candidate helps to build relationships between the baptism family and the church family. It builds owner-ship and personal welcome from the church to the family and the candidate too.

If appropriate, there may be a point in the service where some of the messages might be read out for people to hear, as a prayer for the future life of the candidate on the day of their baptism.

Godparent letter  **Allow 10 minutes**

> **You will need:**
> Pieces of paper; pens

This activity involves creating a memory of the baptism day, which is a special thing to do. It is important to enable a family to capture some of the wonder of the day so that it is not lost after the event. Godparents form an important part of the service when the candidates are very young, and choosing a godparent is a careful decision.

Encourage the candidate, if they are old enough (or the parents, if the candidate is too young), to write a letter to the godparents.

The letter could say why these godparents have been chosen (reasons might include family connections and friendship, but they could also include the particular gifts that might make them good godparents for the candidate), what the candidate will look for in the godparents, and how the godparents can fulfil their role, both on the day of the baptism and in the future.

It would also be fantastic to ask godparents to write a responding letter, saying why they agreed to be a godparent and what it means for them. They can describe what they intend to do to fulfil their role. (This could also be done by email or text.)

Encourage plenty of interaction between those who will be undertaking a special role on and beyond the day of the baptism.

The service  Allow 10 minutes

> **You will need:**
> The baptism symbols (water, cross, candle and so on)

All the preparation and anticipation leads up to the service itself. This is the time when the family, the candidate and the church family gather in the presence of God to respond to his love with this ancient tradition of water, the cross and the light of Christ. It is a tradition that has been followed for many hundreds of years and many millions of times across the world. The ritual, in its essence, speaks of its history and its significance. The symbolism involved is able to speak for itself.

Allow the group enough space and time to explore the symbolism of baptism. Part of your aim for the day is to enable the candidate and their family to engage with the history and mystery of the sacrament of baptism. Rather than feeling the need to have everything explained, it is about allowing them to experience something and, through the experience, to catch a glimpse of the wonder of God at a special moment in a special place.

For those who administer baptism, it is important to understand that we will enable this glimpse to be seen most clearly when we too are open to it. In baptism, enjoy the awe and wonder of this special ministry and enjoy the moments of joy and silence, stillness and depth that occur during the service.

Biography  Allow 10 minutes

> **You will need:**
> Photos of the baptism family/media file; photos of the church family/ media file

Ask the family to create a short biography of the candidate and of the family they are part of. They could do this with photos, or the biography could be written or spoken; it could even be on PowerPoint or on a media file. The biography could be used to introduce the candidate and their family to the church family.

The church family should also produce a biography, to be shown to the family at the baptism, when the two biographies are exchanged. The church biography should show the family why it is good to be baptised into this church family. It would be the ideal place, too, to advertise church events or places where the family might become more part of the fellowship. There may be toddler groups to advertise, or family services, Christmas activities and social events. It should also be a place where the church is able to show how it will fulfil its promise of welcome to those who are baptised.

It would be tempting to make the church biography into a large and unwieldy document, but try to keep it short. Make it welcoming to the family and use it as an opportunity for the church to blow its own trumpet. It can also be a helpful activity to get the church thinking through how it welcomes baptism families and what there is, or what there could be, for those who might come to church. It could be the start of a mission audit.

Once the service is complete, do not think of it as the end. The service is just the focus through which a new life begins. It is easy to enjoy good relationships with a candidate and their family while preparing for the service and on the day itself, only to lose touch when the church door closes. There is much more to be done in maintaining relationships and enabling those who have been baptised to grow in faith and in community. Baptism is for life, not just the christening.

Party on!

Session aim

To explore the themes of life after baptism—the longer-term development of those baptised, following on from baptism and living as a disciple.

Setting the scene

For the family and for the church congregation, it is very easy to see the baptism service as the goal to which all the preparation moves. The family will set a date for the service and the party, send out invitations and gather the wider family together. The service could be the highlight of the day, although, for some, the highlight will be the reception afterwards. This day of being together as a family should be a day to remember, but it should not be seen as an end, the completion of a task, but rather as the start of a new life.

Weddings can sometimes feel the same for a couple. They work towards the special date and share a wonderful day together. It can be easy to forget that the wedding is not the end of all the preparation but, rather, the beginning, the door into married life.

Baptism is a door into a new way of life. It is a recognition of God's part in our lives. The promises made in the baptism service speak not just of the moment but of the way of life ahead. Those coming to church for baptism should be encouraged and enabled to understand this reality. Sadly, too often the church also falls into the mindset of viewing the baptism as the end.

We can become lazy in expecting people neither to return to church nor to invest in the spiritual life that they have committed themselves to in the baptism service. This attitude does us no credit and often tarnishes the way we prepare for baptisms and minister within them.

The future life of those we contact through baptism should be as important as the preparations we make for the day itself. We should seek to give people practical skills to continue the development of their spiritual lives. We should seek to engage people with the church and the life of faith. These encouragements should enable people to begin from wherever their starting point may be, and to take steps forward in faith and awareness of the promises and presence of God.

We will look at blessing, exploring the gifts of baptism. These gifts may have been recognised on the day, in the service, but in this session we consider how families might continue to celebrate them. At some weddings and baptisms, people receive presents that they do not open on the special day itself. Time may not be available in the day, with all the celebrations, to unwrap the gifts they have been given. This activity takes place after the day itself, extending the celebration and bringing joy and wonder at people's generosity and good wishes. Exploring the gifts of baptism should be no different: memories of the day, mementos and activities, rituals and the development of new family traditions will assist in the continuing exploration of what began with the baptism build-up and celebration.

At the baptism service, the family and candidate recognised and acknowledged the presence of God. We would hope that the depth of this awareness of God was genuine and inspiring. For those who are not used to thinking about God, it can seem more natural to do so in the church building, on a special day. Enabling people to consider the presence of God in their daily lives beyond the church walls is surely a crucial task of the church. Perhaps this is a more important element of our mission than our desire to see people return to the church building in the future. If we can enable people to look for and recognise God's presence in the world, if we can give people skills and confidence to attend to God in their lives, that is successful mission.

Continuing relationships are important too, helping people to nurture these new gifts and giving them support and care. One of our aims should always be to continue the relationship between those baptised, their family and the church. We can be too quick to judge those who come for baptism and then never attend again, but perhaps we need to look at ourselves too. Perhaps we are too quick to visit a family requesting a baptism and then never visit again until they call for us.

As well as ideas to explore a continuation of the baptism journey, this session also offers strategies and plans for realistically and successfully continuing links with baptism families.

Baptism in New Testament times meant the start of discipleship, and this must be our aim too. We should seek to support, enable, encourage and enthuse those who come for baptism so that they may begin a life of discipleship. We must be prepared to be used by God to walk with the people he calls, and to see this ministry as vital—life-giving to those we meet, to the church and to the mission of God.

Session activities

In Session 3, there are fewer 'mains' and 'starters'. These could be used as part of the baptism preparation before the service itself, to highlight the long-term nature of baptism; or to enable those coming for baptism to think about what happens after the date of the service; or at a gathering after the baptism service (perhaps a follow-up visit, a gathering of those who have been baptised, or a service giving thanks for all the baptisms in the church).

The majority of the ideas in Session 3 are 'desserts', activities for those baptised and their families to explore together. There are also activities and strategies for the church to consider as ways to keep in contact with baptism families and encourage them to grow in faith and into church life.

Main course

Option 1: God is everywhere!   Allow 20–30 minutes

You will need:
A collection of pictures (postcards, newspapers, magazines) that suggest the presence of God

Look through the pictures, identifying those that suggest the presence of God—perhaps through the beauty of creation or in the wonder of relationships. Encourage people to be as creative as possible in seeing God in the images they find. Explore what God might wish to say to us about the images: what would God think about the world and the people in the images? If God were looking at the images with us, what would he be saying?

When looking at the images, it will be useful to start with positive pictures of the wonder of creation and the goodness of human relationships. If possible, though, it would be good to find the right moment to consider some more difficult themes. Newspapers will often show images in which the presence of God may be more difficult to see. These are important elements to explore. We hope that the day of the baptism will be like the positive pictures, but lifelong faith will encounter many days when God will seem further away. It is crucial to develop this theme in preparation.

Find two pictures in a magazine or newspaper, one that is a positive picture of the world and one that is not. Write down what you think God says about the events going on in the images. This could also present an opportunity to write about our own experiences (good times when God seems close, difficult times when he seems far away, and other times when he seems close again). This would highlight that our perception of God's closeness changes but God is always with us.

Starters you can use with Option 1 main

- How was the baptism?
- Where are they now?

Desserts you can use with Option 1 main

- Baptism letter
- Keeping in touch with godparents
- How to pray

Option 2: Squeeze

 Allow 5–10 minutes

No equipment is needed for this activity

This is a very simple activity, which can be used to consider how people enter the family of the church at baptism, and how each person has a role to play in the life of the church. Consider what gifts and talents each person has and how they might use them in church life. Ensure that you follow up on any offers: if someone feels that their talent is not valued, they may not be willing to offer again.

Form a circle and hold hands. The leader should squeeze the hand of the person to their right. That person, feeling the squeeze, should then squeeze the hand of the next person to their right, and so on until the squeeze returns to the person who sent it. This activity has a multitude of variations. Try it with the circle facing outwards or with eyes closed. Different people could start the squeeze on its journey.

The squeeze can be used to explore how each person plays their part in the whole. If one person is not present in the circle, then the squeeze ceases its journey. That affects not only the person who missed it but all those who would have followed, too.

This activity can also be used to explore the means by which the gospel story and the tradition of baptism have been passed down from generation to generation. Each person has played their part. Who told you? How did you decide to come to baptism? Who will you tell in the future? Explore how people will continue the momentum of the baptism squeeze.

If you are working on the baptism with an individual or a small family, this activity could be done in the baptism service. It could be used in the sermon slot, during the Peace, or at the end as part of the blessing. These variations enable it to be used several times with a different slant, each time giving further opportunities to explore the themes it develops.

It is great fun in a church, trying to form a chain of people. It will usually be impossible to create a circle including everyone, but encourage people to link up with their neighbours. This way, the snake of the chain will wind around the church and everyone will be involved. Getting everyone linked in is an activity in itself and strengthens the message.

Starters you can use with Option 2 main
- How was the baptism?
- Granny went shopping

Desserts you can use with Option 2 main
- Church membership
- Keeping in touch with godparents
- Use your baptism candle
- Plant something

Option 3: Facebook page  Allow 20–30 minutes

You will need:
Access to a Facebook profile page; flipchart showing a larger version to collate responses; pens; laptop/computer linked to OHP equipment, with Facebook access (optional)

This activity explores our ongoing relationship with God.

Before the exercise, look at the current format of a Facebook profile page. You may find it useful to make a note of the information to be submitted and create a larger version on a flipchart to write down your group's agreed responses. If someone in your group is good with computers, you may be able to use a computer linked to a projector so that everyone can see.

Create an imaginary Facebook account for God (there is no need to create an actual account). Look at the information required when setting up a Facebook account and, together, work out what answers God might enter. There is much food for discussion in this exercise. What is God's age? What would God's profile picture be? What about his family members and friends? Encourage discussion on each answer, and do not censor suggestions. Take the opportunity to listen and learn about people's perceptions of God.

Highlight the links to the *My Baptism Journey* activity book with the following questions: Why are you being baptised? Who will you tell about your baptism?

There is an opportunity here to discuss how God keeps in contact with his friends and maintains or conducts relationships. There is also the chance to talk about prayer, to highlight that not only can we speak with God but he will also speak with us. What might people write on his timeline, and what might his comments be about what we write on ours? On a Facebook page, people are encouraged to answer the question 'What is on your mind?' How fascinating it may be to discuss what your group members think might be on God's mind, and to hear their ideas on what God might think regarding what is on their minds.

Highlight the reality that our relationship with God in baptism is not about just one day, but is about every moment of our lives, for all of our lives.

Starters you can use with Option 3 main
- Where are they now?
- How was the baptism?

Desserts you can use with Option 3 main
- Baptism letter
- Keeping in touch with godparents
- How to pray

Option 4: Disciples

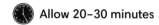 Allow 20–30 minutes

No equipment is needed for this activity

This activity is a wonderful opportunity to develop relationships between those who have come to the church for the baptism and the regular congregation. There is also something wonderful about giving church members confidence to talk about their faith. The whole congregation can be encouraged when they see candidates learning about the long-term implications for living out baptism promises.

Look together at how people follow God through the good and bad times of life. One way to do this would be to ask members of the church congregation to speak about their experiences of God in their lives. It may be useful for them to relate how God can feel close and far off in life, and how they develop in faith through hard times and good times.

People who have come for baptism on previous occasions could be invited back to tell those who have just celebrated their baptism how things have gone since their own big day. Failing that, you could look through the lives of the twelve apostles and the women who followed Jesus. Tell some of their stories, and wonder how their experience of God may have changed and developed over their lives. Consider the ups and downs, the feeling of being close to God and the feeling of being far from him.

This main course is all about faith as a journey. Take time to develop the things which can help in this journey, including the wonders of exploring the Bible, being part of the church, fellowship with other Christians and prayer. This may prove to be the place where people can ask questions they have never felt able to ask before.

For the activity to work well, all the participants will need to feel relaxed and at ease. Work hard on hospitality and welcome when using it as part of a session together.

Starters you can use with Option 4 main
- How was the baptism?
- Granny went shopping

Desserts you can use with Option 4 main
- Baptism letter
- Keeping in touch with godparents
- How to pray
- Plant something

Option 5: Praying

 Allow 20–30 minutes

You will need:
(Depending on what you choose to do) Appropriate items to help prompt prayer (perhaps baptism symbols)

This is a wonderful activity to help develop relationships between those who have come to the church for the baptism and the regular congregation. There is also something wonderful about encouraging church members to express their faith through praying together. For the activity to work well, all the participants will need to feel relaxed and at ease. Work hard on hospitality and welcome when using it as part of a session together.

Give people an opportunity to pray. Model prayer so that others see how it can be done, but highlight that there are different ways to pray. If you are working in a group, there are many ways to model and teach prayer. Here are some suggestions:

- **Circle prayer:** Explain quickly that we are going to say our prayers together, taking turns to pray; make sure everyone knows the order. Describe how people sometimes pray out loud and sometimes pray silently inside. Say that each person should say 'Amen' when they finish their prayer so that the next person knows to begin theirs. You, as the leader, begin and lead with a very short and simple prayer: 'Thank you for these people, for our time together and for our baptism. Amen.' The next person then says their short prayer, and the prayers move around the circle. This very simple format has been used in many settings and has enabled many people to take their first steps in prayer.
- **Using objects:** Prayers do not need to be in words. Taking time to pick up and respond to physical objects (for example, some of the baptism symbols) can also enable people to reflect prayerfully on God.

- **Using passages from the Bible**: Reading and responding to some of the scriptures (such as favourite psalms, the Lord's Prayer, or stories on the baptism theme) can lead naturally to a time of reflection and prayer in a group or individually.
- **Nurturing a regular prayer life**: Prayer is a wonderful thing. It can take many forms, but we often fail to nurture it in those who come to church. In prayer, there is both talking to God and listening to God. Prayer is asking God about the things on our minds and saying 'thank you' for good things and 'sorry' for the things we do wrong. Prayer can be noisy, silent, active and peaceful. Most of all, though, prayer should be something we do rather than something we think we do, or something we think we ought to do.

Starters you can use with Option 5 main
- How was the baptism?
- Granny went shopping

Desserts you can use with Option 5 main
- Baptism letter
- Keeping in touch with godparents
- How to pray
- Plant something

 Starters

How was the baptism?　　　　　 Allow 10 minutes

No equipment is needed for this activity

This is the most important starter for Session 3, and should perhaps be chosen before any other starter or main course.

Take time to ask people how the baptism went from their point of view. Did they enjoy the day? Be interested in their experience of the service. Do not judge their answers, but learn from them. Do not seek to defend things that you may need to reconsider, but be encouraged by compliments and thanks.

Simple questions to use when opening this conversation might be:

- What was your favourite part of the baptism?
- Which bit of the service will you remember most?
- What was the most important thing for you about the baptism service?
- Which bit of the service was the most special?
- Which bit was the most unusual or odd?
- Is there anything you didn't understand or wanted to ask about?

Where are they now?

 Allow 10 minutes

You may need:
Pieces of paper; pens

This starter is ideal when introducing the importance of staying in touch after the baptism. It opens the topic of how the role of the godparents continues beyond the day of the baptism. It is also useful when considering the long-term nature of baptism, following on from the service.

Think together about people you have known in the past who you are no longer in contact with. Where might they be now? What might they be doing in their lives? If you met them now, what would you ask them? What would you wish to tell them about yourself?

If you are speaking with a family who are preparing a baby for baptism, talk about things that they would like the baby to know about when they are old enough to understand. What is it about the baptism that the family would like them to know? Perhaps it would be appropriate to write some messages together to be given to the baby when they are, say, ten years old (or perhaps 21). In the letter, say what happened at the baptism and why it was so important for the family to be there. Write down your hopes for the child's future, when they receive the letter.

This is an ideal opportunity to encourage parents to describe some way in which the godparents may help and support their child. Create a good place for this discussion to take place, and enable godparents to understand and agree to try to fulfil the role they are being asked to undertake.

Granny went shopping

 **Allow 10 minutes**

No equipment is needed for this activity

This is a very simple memory game. It is perfect for introducing themes of consequences, of everyone playing their part, and the sense that baptism is a journey and not just a service.

The game is easiest to play in a circle. The first person begins by saying, 'My granny went shopping and she bought a ...' and adding an item that Granny could have bought at the shops (for example, 'My granny went shopping and she bought a cucumber').

The next person in the circle repeats the sentence and adds a new purchase. So they might say, 'My granny went shopping and she bought a cucumber and a saucepan.' The next person repeats the growing shopping list and adds a new item. So the list grows and grows, with people trying to remember what has been bought by Granny.

This style of game is also ideal as a way of introducing names when a new group meets. Again, a circle is a good formation where possible. The host introduces themselves: 'I'm Tina.' Then they ask the next person to introduce them again, and to add their own name. So it might be, 'This is Tina, and I'm James.' The next person introduces all the people before them and adds their own name.

With large groups, this is a great way to get people to remember names and also a way of enabling the group to work together, as it soon becomes a test not only for the next individual in the circle but also for the whole group. The game should always end with the host (who started the game with the easiest task of merely introducing themselves) making a joke of congratulating the person who had to remember everybody. It is fun to suggest that the activity should end there, but often the group will demand that the host have a go at the whole lot. The host should always give it a try.

 Desserts

Baptism letter

 Allow 20 minutes

You will need:
(Depending on what you decide to do) Pieces of paper; pens; alternative forms of recording people's thoughts (such as email, text or MP3)

This activity is designed to highlight the journey element of baptism and can be used to enable people to talk through what happened on the day and to reflect upon it. It is also a great activity to maintain contact with baptism families beyond the service itself.

Encourage people to write a letter just after the baptism. In the letter, they should write about what happened at the baptism and what their thoughts were about the day. What was their favourite thing about it? What was most important? How did being baptised make them feel? What do they think they will most remember? In the letter, they should write the promises that were made and write about how they will try to keep them.

Encourage them to seal the letter in an envelope and give it to someone who will keep it (without looking at it) for a year and return it to them on the anniversary of their baptism.

This activity is perfect for young people and adults to complete on their own. For babies who are being baptised, the godparents or parents can write the letter.

There are opportunities at other points in the baptism preparation to write different letters. For example, when the baptism is booked, it may be useful to encourage people to write a letter to themselves about what they are expecting and looking forward to.

For those who are less used to writing letters, find an appropriate method of capturing people's thoughts, perhaps by email, text or MP3 file. It may be that people will talk and you write their words down. The key element is to keep a record of people's thoughts and feelings on the date of writing; these can then be reviewed and reflected on at a later date.

Keeping in touch with godparents  Allow 20 minutes

You may need:
Pieces of paper; pens

This activity is designed to enable families and godparents to consider how they will continue in their baptismal responsibilities beyond the date of the baptism itself. It gives people an opportunity to share good ideas and talk together about the future.

Ask your group to share ideas in twos and threes about how they will keep in touch. Each subgroup should talk about what the parents would like the godparents to do for their godchild in the future.

Following this discussion, people should move around and have a new discussion on the same topic. To begin with, they should share good ideas from the previous discussion and then come up with some new ideas. Further moving around into new groups can continue until time is up or the activity needs bringing together. The activity should end by collating the ideas that people thought were good ones for everyone to remember.

Some groups may find it less comfortable to talk together. If so, ask the group to sit in a circle; give each person a piece of paper and ask them to write down their answers to the above questions (the crucial questions are about what parents would like godparents to do, and how godparents will try to keep in touch). When each person has written an idea, they should pass the paper to the next person, who can add an idea to the list. The lists can continue round until each person has their own returned to them. (If their own idea has already been listed by someone else, they should try to think of a second good idea, but they should only need three or four ideas, even in quite a large group.)

Where baptism visits are performed with individual families or in homes, this activity can still be done usefully. The person visiting should maintain a list of good ideas for godparents from parents who have chosen them, and a list of ways godparents have suggested that they can keep in touch with their godchildren. This list could be given to parents and godparents, and they can be encouraged to add a new suggestion to the list.

This discussion enables people to consider the long-term relationship that is begun through the baptism and to talk about what they are expecting of each other. It sets out an open expectation within the family.

The keeping of the list enables good ideas to be passed on, and new families are encouraged to think for themselves too. It may be that a new list needs to be started every so often.

How to pray

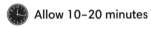 **Allow 10–20 minutes**

You will need:
(Depending on what you choose to do) Objects to prompt prayer; a 'sacred space' set up for your group to pray in

This activity is about enabling those who are baptised to continue in a journey of discipleship and faith. In general, the church has not had a good reputation for enabling people to attend to God in prayer. When we baptise people, it is important that we give them some skills in prayer and open to them the myriad ways that this relationship of prayer may develop.

When speaking about prayer, it is crucial to model a variety of ways in which it can be done. Do not feel you have to model them all but do try to offer a good variety of methods. Make sure the different methods of prayer you use have a wide spread of characteristics: they should not all require people to be seated or to be silent. Make sure, too, that the methods you suggest give people practical suggestions. It is not realistic to suggest 15 minutes of quiet, as a first step, to most families who have not been used to praying before.

Those who are not used to prayer can sometimes be unsure of what to say. Churches have often modelled prayer as something that needs to be said in grand, old-fashioned words. Some people will only know the Lord's Prayer in its traditional form as their template for prayer. Others may not know any prayers by heart and may be unsure what words are appropriate. The way this activity works is to model prayer. Consider the ways in which you pray and how you might pass them on to others. Here are some principles and ideas you could use.

- **What is prayer?** It is important to help people to understand what prayer is before you model it. Do not necessarily assume they know nothing, but first listen to their thoughts. Don't judge their response but listen carefully, for, by understanding what they think, you can work with them and enable them to develop their prayer life. Some elements to consider together are about being aware of God's presence, bringing ourselves before God, speaking to God and listening to him.

- **Praying in a circle:** If you are in a group, this is an ideal setting for enabling people to pray. A family home will be just as good a place to show people how they can pray. Rather than praying 'for them' or giving them words to read out in prayer, explain simply that the group or family are all going to pray together: you will start and the person next to you will pray after you. Explain briefly that when it is their turn, each person might pray silently with words inside or pray aloud with spoken words. Make sure each person knows that, whichever way they pray, they just need to say 'Amen' when they are finished so that the next person knows when to start. Then begin. Make your starting prayer very simple: 'God, thank you for this baby, for new life and for a wonderful baptism service. Amen.' Encourage people around the circle, with stillness and silence, to continue the circle of prayer. The model of people's silence and simple words will give others the skill of finding words to use in prayer.
- **Wondering:** Prayer does not necessarily involve words or being still. Prayer may be acknowledging the wonder of God in creation, which might easily include a newborn child. Modelling this form of prayer is very easy in a home visit or a baptism service. Enable people to look at the world around with eyes that give thanks to God. Help people to notice things around them and to be thankful.
- **Finding time:** Time is often the most difficult thing for people (especially new mums) to find. Invite people to think of a time in the day when they can think through what is on their minds—perhaps while cleaning their teeth, walking the dog or even going to the toilet. Encourage them, in that time, to think about the things they are worried about, the things they are thankful for, and people who are on their minds. At the end of thinking through these things, they can say 'Amen'.
- **Creating a sacred space:** The importance of place is useful in encouraging people in their prayer life. A particular part of the house may be set aside for prayer, or a particular seat or a spot under a tree. Special places can be created, too. Collecting special items together can make part of a room a dedicated place for prayer. Flowers, photographs, a cross or other items could be useful.
- **Using prayer objects:** Make a prayer cube, with a different short prayer written on each of the six faces. Roll the cube and say the prayer on the top face. Objects like this can help people find time and encouragement to pray.

These are a few things to consider as you work with those who may have little experience of prayer. Others may be more confident in prayer, and there will be other suggestions to make from your own knowledge and the life of the church. It is important that church begins again to enable people to pray. We have not been good at this in the past, and we should not be nervous of giving people courage and confidence in this wonderful skill. Especially with a family or person who is coming to us for baptism, why should we be nervous of speaking with them about prayer and enabling them to do it?

Church membership
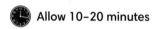 **Allow 10–20 minutes**

You may need:
Pieces of paper; pens

This activity is about encouraging those who are baptised to recognise and develop their part in the church. Baptism is a sacrament that holds not only personal significance to the one being baptised but is also about membership in the family of the church. People are not baptised in isolation. Baptism is about becoming a child of God and a fellow heir with others who are in the community of faith, so it is important that those who are baptised should be welcomed and encouraged to get involved in the church community. Here are some ideas to explore in your group:

- **Preparing others:** Mums and their children can often be a source of enthusiasm for welcoming others. Why not ask those who have had their children baptised to help prepare the next family that brings a baby for baptism? This will create stronger relationships and confidence in faith.
- **Using people's gifts:** People of all ages bring gifts into the church. There will be people asking for baptism who could help with welcoming, music, IT and coffee. While making sure that you do not overwhelm them immediately by asking them to be on all the rotas, enable them to find a place to use their talents and become part of the church community.
- **Be welcoming:** If a baptism is a first-time or a very rare visit to church, it is important to enable the baptism family to be part of the church. It may be difficult for them to get to church every week, but once a month might be a manageable starting point. If that is a step too far, invite them specifically to Christmas and Easter services. If people start to enjoy church and realise

that they are able to make it part of their life, then they may be encouraged to come more often. Make it easy for people to join in and get to the services (for example, perhaps lift-sharing can be arranged). Never be annoyed if they do not come, but rejoice when they come through the doors. If people don't come for a while, notice when they are missing—not in a judgmental way but out of concern for them.

Use your baptism candle

 Allow 10 minutes to introduce

You may need:
A baptism candle; matches

Many churches give a baptism candle to those who are baptised. It signifies the light of Christ into which we have come at baptism. Often we suggest that people should light it on the anniversary of the baptism—but that is a whole year away. The candle may be the only tangible and interactive resource that a family receives from the baptism, so it is vital that they are encouraged to use it. The presence of the candle may enable the light of the baptism to shine in the house long after the family have left the church building. If the candle is kept in a drawer as a memento, this may reflect the way faith is also viewed by the family, but the seed of faith and the candle will always have the potential to shine again in God's time. This activity explores how to use the baptism candle to nurture faith.

Straight after the baptism, suggest that the candle is lit again later in the day—perhaps at lunchtime or before bedtime—to remind the family to think about and give thanks for the day and for the baptism. When it is lit, remember how the day has felt, and be thankful for family and friends, for fun and the baptism service.

When lighting the candle, make it a special moment. See how the light of the candle grows; see how it dispels the darkness; see how it is warm and alive, and think about how this reflects the light of Christ which was given at baptism.

When extinguishing the light, notice how the smoke leaves the candle. It is almost as if the light has been released from the wick and set free. It gets thinner and thinner until it cannot be seen. We shine with the light of Christ and we too must not let our light be stuck in one place; it should be free for people to see. Think about how you can show the light of Christ in your life by what you do for other people.

Light the candle again a week later. Again, think about the baptism service. What was happening this time last week? What do you remember most? A week later, what do you think was the most important thing about the day?

Encourage the family to use the candle in this way to rekindle the memory of the baptism. Its light will continue to shine. Perhaps the candle can be used at birthdays, each Sunday, or once each month and then on the anniversary too. If it is not used for a year, it may never see the light of day again, but, if it burns out because it has been so well used, then it has served a greater purpose.

Water thinking Allow 10 minutes to introduce

You may need:
Water (as an interactive visual aid)

Just as the candle was used in the previous activity to enable the baptism to be remembered and its message retold, the family could be encouraged to remember the baptism whenever they use water. Here are some ideas to discuss in your group:

- **Bath time:** This can be a point in the day when the family remembers what happened at the font. Sprinkling water can be used to remember how the baptismal waters bring cleaning and new life.
- **Pouring water:** Water from the tap can call to mind the refreshing water of baptism. It is an image that the family should be encouraged to remember and talk about.
- **Interacting with children:** If there are children in the baptismal family, encourage the adults to talk with them about what happened at the baptism service. Then it is for the adults to listen, and together the family can explore how spectacular the water of baptism can be.

Plant something Allow 10–20 minutes

You may need:
Something to plant (seeds, bulbs, a shrub or a tree); somewhere to plant it (a pot of soil or an appropriate spot in the garden); relevant gardening equipment (and prompts to water, nurture, and check up on its growth)

Sometimes the preparations for a baptism service can make the event itself feel like an ending; it becomes the culmination of all the planning. Baptism, though, is very much a beginning, the start of a journey, a new life. Why not plant something to signify this new start? Here are some suggestions:

- For fast results, cress or mustard is ideal.
- For a longer-term project, bulbs are good.
- For larger spaces, a tree would be a brilliant reminder of a special day and the life and journey that began there.

A special note for the godparents  Allow 10 minutes

You may need:
Pieces of paper; pens

We hope that being chosen as a godparent will have been seen as a great privilege, and that they too will have enjoyed being part of this special day. It truly is an honour and a responsibility that goes well beyond the day itself, so encourage godparents to consider what they will do, beyond the day of the baptism. Here are some ideas to explore in your group:

- **Pray:** The most important thing that godparents can do is to pray for the child they have supported and spoken for at the baptism. Encourage them to talk to God about the child, giving thanks for their gifts and talents. If the child goes through difficult times, they can pray for them to be given strength or peace, that they may find a way through their trouble. When the child is in good times, they can be thankful and give thanks for things to celebrate, like good results, success in sport or school work, fun and happy days. At baptism, the godparents gave thanks for this child's wonderful creation, remembering that God created them and promises his love for them. Encourage godparents to talk to God about the things the child goes through day to day as they grow up, and inspire them not to let the praying stop. They can look forward to praying for the child in their relationships and careers. People say you never stop being a parent, and that goes for godparents too.
- **Keep in touch:** The godparents were chosen by the child's parents to watch over the child's spiritual and life development. To do this, they will need to keep in contact with the family and be aware of what is going on for them.

Encourage godparents to make the most of the many good times along the way, not waiting for bad times before thinking that they have something to do. Godparents should keep a watch on their godchildren, asking regularly about how they are doing and how things are for them. They have been chosen to do this, so they should neither feel embarrassed about doing it nor forget to do it.

- **Get good gifts:** There will be times when godparents may be able to send a gift to their godchildren. Anniversaries of the baptism, birthdays, Christmas and Easter all give a chance to send or give something to them. Suggest that godparents think carefully about the gifts they might give. They could try to give something that reflects what happened on the day of the baptism—something about God, a Bible, a book of prayers or a cross. They could give something that is special to the child, something with their name on or something that they are collecting or doing as a hobby. They could give something that costs nothing, such as time to play together or go for a walk in a park. Godparents could talk to their godchildren about the day of the baptism and how special it is for them to be their godparent, and what the day meant for them. Maybe godparent and godchild could look together at photos from the day and light the baptism candle together when they remember the special day.

Downloadable appendices

✛

Planning sheet

Preparation	
What preparations do I need to make (for example, for a group session or an informal meeting with candidates or their parents)?	
Session or visit plan	
What is the setting? A baptism class/ A session with a children's group/ A church leadership group/ A visit to a candidate's family/ Other	
How long will my session/visit need?	
What equipment/materials do I need?	
Will I need to hand out the *My Baptism Journey* activity book in this setting?	
Is there anything else I need to consider?	

Menu		
What starters will I use?	What mains will I use?	What desserts will I use?

Reflections on the session
(complete immediately afterwards)

- How did the group respond to the activities?

- What adaptations did I make to the activities?

- What went well?

- What did I learn that will be useful for planning in the future?

- Has the content of this session made me think about anything in particular?

✠

Reflection sheet

Session	Activity/Questions
	What are the key areas for me in this session?
	What challenged me in this session?
	What would I like to explore more, and how will I go about it?
	Is there anything I would like to pray about?

Reproduced with permission from *Getting Ready for Baptism* by Richard Burge, Penny Fuller and Mary Hawes (Barnabas for Children, 2014) www.barnabasforchildren.org.uk

Work sheet

God the Father

The Bible begins and ends with God's love: in the beginning is the story of creation, and in the end he sent his only Son. The most important thing to remember is that God's love is not limited, and it is not blind. The more we accept God's love, the more we are able to love others.

- Read the passage: Luke 15:4–7.
- The extent to which God loves us: The parable of the lost sheep.

What is Jesus telling us about God?

Jesus the Son of God

'This man really was the Son of God!' (Mark 15:39). Jesus turned the values of the world upside down. He called people to live for God, and he opened the door for us to find our way back to God.

- Read the passage: Luke 3:21–22.
- Jesus was baptised by John the Baptist.

Why do you think Jesus wanted to be baptised?

God the Holy Spirit

The Holy Spirit is a powerful energy that comes from God and is a gift for us. He gives us confidence to live our lives as God wants.

- Read the passage: Acts 13:2–4.
- God sends out Barnabas and Paul.

What do you think it would feel like to drop everything and go where God tells you to go?

John the Baptist

John started preaching before Jesus did. He lived in the desert on his own. Jesus came to him to be baptised. John knew who Jesus was and believed that Jesus should baptise him. John followed his mission from God and baptised Jesus.

- Read the passage: Matthew 3:13–17.

Why do you think John listened to Jesus?

Mary the mother of Jesus

Mary had a deep faith in God and did as God asked of her. She obeyed and trusted in God and supported Jesus.

- Read the passage: Luke 1:28–33.
- Gabriel announces to Mary about Jesus.

How do you think Mary felt about being the mother of Jesus?

Paul

Paul was a Roman citizen born in a Greek town and, like his father, was a Pharisee. Paul was passionate about his religion and was against Christianity until he had a vision from God. Paul was determined that nothing should get in the way of people hearing about the good news.

- Read the passage: Acts 1:8.
- The Holy Spirit speaks to the apostles.

What would you do if this happened to you?

Samuel

Samuel's mother dedicated him to God at an early age and sent him to serve in a shrine. He became the chief prophet of Israel. Samuel saw Israel through a time of change. The people looked to him to tell them what God wanted.

- Read the passage: 1 Samuel 7:3–4.
- Samuel asked the people to dedicate themselves completely to God.

Would it be hard or easy to dedicate yourself completely to God?

Esther

The king of Persia held a beauty contest to find a new queen, and Esther won it. Esther was in the right place at the right time when her people were in trouble. She responded to God's call and had the courage to rescue her people. Esther is a book in the Bible about people who are suffering and oppressed.

- Read the passage: Esther 4:10–16.

What does it mean to be in the right place at the right time?

Deborah

Deborah was a prophet, a wise woman and a leader in Israel. She was a woman with many gifts and skills. She gave advice and settled arguments.

- Read the passage: Judges 5:1–3.
- This is the start of a song Deborah wrote.

What gifts and skills do you have?

Reproduced with permission from *Getting Ready for Baptism* by Richard Burge, Penny Fuller and Mary Hawes (Barnabas for Children, 2014) www.barnabasforchildren.org.uk

Balaam

Balaam was a prophet at the time of King Balak of Moab. He was told to do something he wasn't happy with, and he asked God what to do about it. God said 'Yes, but do exactly as I say.' Balaam headed off on his donkey but didn't see an angel in his path. The donkey swerved out of the way and told Balaam what a fool he was. Balaam eventually arrived at the right place and delivered a prophecy from God.

• Read the passage: Numbers 22—24

Balaam was never really sure of anything. Is it OK to be unsure?

James

James was the younger brother of Jesus and became the leader of the Jewish Christians. His ministry was one of practical action.

• Read the passage: James 2:14–24

What practical action should Christians take in their communities?

Job

Job was a man with a strong faith in God. He was married with lots of children and lived in Uz. He was tested by God and lost everything. Job asked difficult questions about suffering and existence, yet he didn't lose his faith in God.

• Read the passage: Job 24:1–12

What questions do you ask God?

Reproduced with permission from *Getting Ready for Baptism* by Richard Burge, Penny Fuller and Mary Hawes (Barnabas for Children, 2014) www.barnabasforchildren.org.uk

— APPENDIX 4 —

Descriptions of baptism

Read the passages and questions below. They are an exploration of words through art and poetry. Use the questions to help you express your thoughts on paper.

The water of creation

At the very beginning of life itself, we hear how the Spirit of God moved over the waters of creation. Baptism is about a new creation, the start of a new journey of exploration. There are many parallels that can be teased out here.

The parting of the Red Sea

This is a reference that is often used during the baptism service, at the blessing of the water. God brought the people of God through the Red Sea into the promised land. In this story, there are themes of delivery from chaos, rescue, promise, God's presence with his people and his purpose and power in their lives. In baptism, God takes his people through water into the grace of his love.

The promise to Abraham

In the spectacular story of the promise of Isaac, God gives Abraham the promise of a child and a family. His descendants will be more in number than the stars of the sky or the grains of sand in the desert. In baptism, we become one of those stars, a grain of that sand. We become part of the family of the people of God.

Parables

Although none of Jesus' parables is directly about baptism, they talk a lot about the kingdom of God, a theme that can be used in a baptism sermon or in

Reproduced with permission from *Getting Ready for Baptism* by Richard Burge, Penny Fuller and Mary Hawes (Barnabas for Children, 2014) www.barnabasforchildren.org.uk

sessions. A Samaritan who loved his neighbour as himself, servants who used their talents, people invited to celebrations, and sheep that are lost and called by name are among many of the characters in the parables, on themes that can be relevant to those coming for baptism.

Baptism is theological

When Jesus was baptised in the waters of the River Jordan, the Holy Spirit descended upon him like a dove and the voice of God the Father was heard by some who witnessed the event. This is a biblical moment in which we see the wonder of the Trinity, and baptism is a deeply trinitarian event. In the final words of Matthew's Gospel, Jesus instructed the disciples to baptise others in the name of the Father, the Son and the Holy Spirit. While this reference is seen by some to be a later addition to fit with church practice, it reflects the very theocentric element of baptism, which is often forgotten.

Questions
- Where is God?
- What images spring to mind when you read the passages? Express them in colour on your paper.
- What words stand out for you, and how do they make you feel? Write them on your paper.
- Draw whatever strikes you from the above passages.
- Create a poem that reflects one of the passages.

— APPENDIX 5 —

Images of baptism

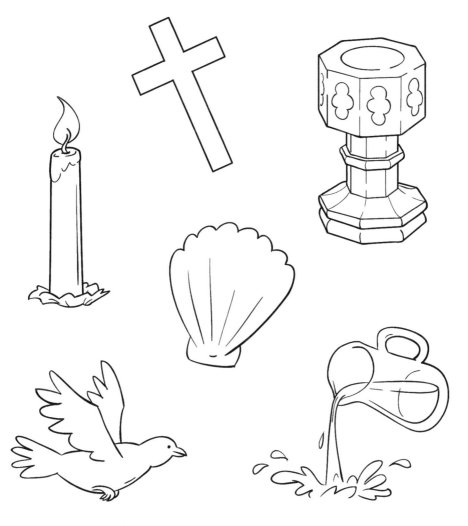

Reproduced with permission from *Getting Ready for Baptism* by Richard Burge, Penny Fuller and Mary Hawes (Barnabas for Children, 2014) www.barnabasforchildren.org.uk

Story cards

Aaron	Abraham (Abram)
Moses' spokesman and his deputy. Once the Israelites had escaped from Egypt, Aaron was appointed high priest. He was specifically chosen by God for a difficult and dangerous job.	Aged 75 when God called him, without any children. God promised to bless Abram and make him a 'great nation'. He left his home when God told him to and travelled many miles. He had faith that God would do what he said he would do.
Esther	**John**
God made Esther a queen so that she could rescue her people. She had the courage to act to save her people, when she could have kept quiet.	The son of elderly parents, and Jesus' cousin, John started preaching before Jesus did. He ate locusts and honey while living in the desert, and he called people to be baptised.
Mary	**Paul**
The mother of Jesus, from a poor family, she had a deep faith, listened to God and trusted him. She had a hard journey with Joseph to Bethlehem and gave birth to Jesus shortly after they arrived.	Believed that Christ had died for everyone and was determined that people should hear about God. He was given immense wisdom and insight from God, which have shaped the church.
Matthew	**Solomon**
One of the tax collectors, who were hated because they worked with the Roman authorities and had a reputation as thieves. Jesus called Matthew away from this life, and he became a disciple.	Succeeded his father David to the throne of Israel. God appeared to him in a dream and offered to grant him one request: Solomon asked for wisdom.

Reproduced with permission from *Getting Ready for Baptism* by Richard Burge, Penny Fuller and Mary Hawes (Barnabas for Children, 2014) www.barnabasforchildren.org.uk

Peter A fisherman with Andrew, James and John. Jesus called Peter to be a 'fisher of people'. His real name was Simon but Jesus called him the 'rock', meaning the foundation of the church.	**Stephen** One of seven people who helped the apostles set up the early church, Stephen performed miracles. People were upset by this and got him arrested. He was stoned to death, becoming the first Christian martyr.
Moses Was asked by God to lead his people out of Egypt. God gave him the Law for the people to live by.	**Samuel** His mother dedicated him to the Lord at an early age and sent him to serve in the shrine at Shiloh. He became the chief prophet of Israel.
Noah God was unhappy with the way people were living. Noah was a good and faithful man. God asked him to build an ark, a huge boat, and to prepare for a big flood. Noah trusted God and followed his instructions.	**Barnabas** When he found God, Barnabas sold all his property and gave the money to the early church. The disciples called him Barnabas because it means 'son of encouragement'. He supported Paul in his ministry with the early church.
God The Father, the Son, and the Holy Spirit, known as the Trinity. With the Holy Spirit, Christianity is a living faith.	**David** The shepherd boy who fought the giant Goliath and became a king. Chosen by God to replace King Saul.
Jesus The Son of God made human, he lived in the power of God and preached peace, forgiveness and reconciliation. He befriended people on the margins of society—the poor, tax collectors and prostitutes. He healed people and did miracles.	**Isaiah** A prophet living in a time of turmoil, Isaiah preached that it was wrong to rely on human solutions to the problems and issues of the time. What really mattered was to stop doing bad things and to ask for forgiveness and trust in God.

Reproduced with permission from *Getting Ready for Baptism* by Richard Burge, Penny Fuller and Mary Hawes (Barnabas for Children, 2014) www.barnabasforchildren.org.uk

Church family activities

Communion: Breaking bread and drinking wine together	Prayer: Intercessions, thanksgiving, praise, liturgical	Singing: Choir, individual, congregation, corporate
Teaching: Sermon, talk	Bible reading: Lectionary reading, Bible study	Worship: Includes everything
Gathering: Making a start, getting ready, calling everyone together	Sending out: Giving us something to go out into the world with	Blessing: A final prayer
Welcome: At the door when we arrive	Conversations: Before, after and during the service	Tea and coffee
Governance meetings	Leadership meetings	Coffee mornings
Luncheon club	Bible study groups	Prayer groups
Café church	Messy Church	Midweek groups for children and young people
Sunday school	Prayer breakfasts	Church fête
Pantomimes	Drama group	Keep fit
Seasonal services; holy days; uniformed groups	Women's groups	Men's groups
Holiday clubs	Caring	Trustworthy
Loving	Supporting	Listening
Pastoral	Committed	Volunteers
Social action	Creative	Living Christian values
Charity giver	Walking the walk	Challenging injustice
Care givers	Community	Global action

Reproduced with permission from *Getting Ready for Baptism* by Richard Burge, Penny Fuller and Mary Hawes (Barnabas for Children, 2014) www.barnabasforchildren.org.uk

Eat	Socialise	Be out in the community
Night shelter	Food bank	Homework club
Assemblies	After- or before-school club	Christian Union
Sports teams	Allotment	Local café
Human	Fallible	Hurting
At peace	Strong	Vulnerable
Searching	Have questions	Doubts
Make mistakes	Humble	Arrogant
Lonely	Give freely of themselves	Confident in who they are
Shy	Strong convictions	Faith
Disciples	Strangers	Who Let The Dads Out?
Toddlers	Crèche	Craft days

Reproduced with permission from *Getting Ready for Baptism* by Richard Burge, Penny Fuller and Mary Hawes (Barnabas for Children, 2014) www.barnabasforchildren.org.uk

About the authors

Richard Burge was born in Hull and was baptised as a baby. He studied econometrics and mathematical economics before following his calling into ordained ministry. After a year in France with the Missions to Seafarers, he trained for ordination at Ridley Hall in Cambridge and has served in York and Wakefield Dioceses. He has been a Diocesan Children's Adviser for over ten years and a priest in nine churches since his ordination. He is married to Heather and enjoys walking their dog, Sally. He has taken over 300 baptisms and has only had eight babies cry (so far!).

Penny Fuller is Children's Development Officer in the Methodist Church's Children and Youth Team, with 30 years' practical experience in ministry with children and young people in her local church. She is a Godly Play Trustee and CURBS Trustee (Children in Urban Situations) and is the Moderator of the Consultative Group of Ministry among Children, a national ecumenical children's ministry group. Penny was on the writing group for More Core Skills for Children's Work *(Barnabas, 2010) and co-wrote* Keepin' It Real, *a CURBS resource for 9–13s, and* Participate!, *a vocational resource for 9–14s (Barnabas for Children, 2012).*

The Revd Mary Hawes is the Church of England National Children's Adviser and has many years' experience as a writer, speaker, thinker and practitioner of work with children. She is continually encouraging the church to think deeply about children and young people.